The American Offensive
Dispatches from the Front

Jack Kerwick

The American Offensive: Dispatches from the Front

STAIRWAY PRESS—SEATTLE

Cover Design by Guy D. Corp
www.GrafixCorp.com

STAIRWAY≡PRESS

www.StairwayPress.com
1500A East College Way #554
Mount Vernon, WA 98273 USA

Contents

Jack Kerwick

INTRODUCTION

I AM A philosopher by trade, my area of specialization being political philosophy. I am also an advocate of a nearly extinct worldview in academia: conservatism. However, in the pages to follow, I hope to make it clear that my conservatism is nearly an extinct species in the contemporary political world as well. These two facts regarding my background—my role as a political philosopher and my conservatism—along with the fact that our times, like all times, pose great challenges, account for why I've spent the last few years addressing popular audiences.

It has been my hope that in bringing to bear clear thinking upon the Politically Correct juggernaut that dominates our culture—including both national parties and virtually every ideology—that we can expose its cognitive and moral bankruptcy for what it is.

This book is a collection of some of my essays that have appeared in a variety of popular publications over the last few years. I have arranged them thematically into five chapters.

The first chapter consists of articles that address the national invasion that we misleadingly refer to as "immigration."

The second chapter is devoted to the topic of religion, both the West's Christian legacy as well as the current conflict with Islam.

In the third chapter, I reveal the corruption of head and heart that now passes for an education in the liberal arts in colleges and universities throughout the country.

The fourth chapter is comprised of essays pertaining to race-related issues and the Racism-Industrial-Complex (RIC) that exists to create and exacerbate these issues.

In the fifth and final chapter, the reader will see that I have been at pains to show that the Republican Party and the so-called "conservative movement" that it purports to represent are anything but *conservative*. In fact, it is but another variant of the leftist, egalitarian, Political Correct ideology that it pretends to resist.

IMMIGRATION AND AMNESTY

THE 1965 IMMIGRATION and Naturalization Act marked a fundamental departure from earlier American immigration policy in at least two respects. First, the law encouraged, and was designed to encourage, non-European peoples to immigrate to America. In this regard, it has proven remarkably successful, as approximately 90% of those who enter the country today hail from the Third World. Many of these immigrants are Hispanics. Second, unlike in the past, when large waves of immigration were followed by lengthy lulls so as to provide time for assimilation, the post-1965 wave of immigration has been relentless. As a consequence of these two facts, the nature of American politics has dramatically changed as Republicans and Democrats labor diligently to cater to the Hispanic vote.

There are still other differences between present and past patterns of immigration. For starters, a salient feature of current immigration to the United States is illegal immigration. This, in turn, has lead Republicans, who are ever desperate to remedy their poor showing among Hispanic voters, to advocate tirelessly along with their Democratic counterparts for "comprehensive immigration reform," which never amounts to anything but amnesty by another name.

In the articles that follow, I expose the deep rooted problems with current immigration policy as well as the disingenuousness of those, particularly self-avowed "conservatives," who call for amnesty while denying that they're doing any such thing.

The Truth about Amnesty

For all sorts of reasons, the "comprehensive immigration reform"—i.e. amnesty—on behalf of which Marco Rubio and a whole lot of other Republicans in Washington and "the conservative" media have been advocating from the time of Barack Obama's reelection is a sham and a disaster.

But these Republicans have convinced themselves that, given the ever growing Hispanic segment of the electorate, their party's survival depends upon it.

Some of us have always suspected that the influence of Hispanics over our politics has been greatly exaggerated by those who *want* for Hispanics to achieve more influence, or at least to be perceived as having done so.

Thanks to the Census Bureau's recently released findings, we now know that we have been right all along.

Exit polling data from last year's election revealing that Hispanics constitute 10 percent of the electorate was mistaken. In reality, Hispanics are slightly above 8 percent of the voting public. As writer Steve Sailer remarks:

> So the standard story you've been hearing in the MSM ["Mainstream Media"] for almost seven months is indeed inflated by 19 percent.

It wasn't Hispanics that propelled Obama to victory, but blacks. In fact, even more blacks came out to support Obama in 2012 than did so in 2008. As Sailer says, "blacks added another 10 percent to their vote total from 2008 to 2012. Nationally, 66.2 percent of eligible blacks voted compared to 64.1 percent of whites, 48.0 percent of Hispanics, and 47.3 percent of Asians."

Sailer continues:

> The growth in black turnout was particularly

> *concentrated among those over age 65. Also, black*
> *women traditionally vote at significantly higher*
> *rates than black men, and the black gender gap in*
> *turnout hit a new record in 2012.*

This is significant, for as Sailer observes, the phenomenon of elderly black women seeking "to keep the White House black" is not exactly "the wave of the future." At the very least, it certainly doesn't call for anything along the lines of "comprehensive immigration reform."

In fact, even the Hispanic vote doesn't call for this.

All of the hype regarding the alleged Hispanicization of American politics aside, Hispanic voter turnout was actually *down* in 2012. Sailer asserts:

> *Among Hispanics eligible to vote, gross numbers*
> *continued to rise—but the rate of those taking the*
> *trouble to vote dropped from 49.9 to 48.0 percent.*

Furthermore:

> *The number of Hispanics who claimed to be eligible*
> *but didn't bother to get to the polls soared from*
> *9.8 million to 12.1 million.*

Compared to many of his fellow partisans, to say nothing of his Democratic rival, Mitt Romney was a hard-liner on the immigration problem. Yet, pace those of Romney's critics who swore that this stance of his would cost him the election among Hispanics, the latter actually showed up at the polls in fewer numbers than before.

Yet it isn't just the upsurge in blacks voting for Obama that accounted for Romney's defeat. Romney still could've prevailed—had the rate of white turnout not been at record lows.

It is worth quoting at length Sailer's summary of the Census Bureau's findings:

> *In contrast to the fervent black effort to re-elect Obama, whites were strikingly unmotivated by Romney. The total white vote dropped from 100 million in 2008 to 98 million in 2012 (down 2 percent). Only 64.1 percent of eligible whites voted in 2012, down from 66.1 percent in 2008 and 67.2 percent in the recent high-water mark year of 2004.*

Last year was "the first time in the history of the Census survey that whites were not the highest-ranking group in terms of their rate of voting."

The Census Bureau's findings suggest a few things.

First, the relentless and rapid rise of Hispanic political power is a myth.

Second, the idea that Republicans can capitalize on this power only by supporting amnesty is a myth.

Third, in promoting these myths, the establishment media proves itself once again to be less than entirely trustworthy.

Finally, if Republicans want to win more elections, they should worry less about engaging in self-defeating pandering to minorities and more about stopping the hemorrhaging of their ever-shrinking white base.

Amnesty Nonsense

Let's be blunt: anyone who endorses anything remotely resembling the "comprehensive immigration reform" currently bandied about in Congress is either a fool or a liar.

Amnesty—and make no mistakes about it, "comprehensive immigration reform," "a pathway to citizenship," and whatever other euphemisms its apologists invoke do nothing to change the fact that it *is* amnesty that they favor—is a fool's errand of epic proportions. This becomes obvious once we consider it in light of an analogy from everyday life.

You're married. Chief among the obligations inherent in marriage is that of fidelity. Now, your spouse has chronically failed to fulfill this most basic of duties. Finally, you've had enough.

Upon threatening your philandering spouse with divorce, she acknowledges that your marriage is *broken* before swearing to not only change, but change *radically*. Not only will she stop cheating, she promises to transform herself into the epitome of the subservient, loyal, and loving wife.

While you would doubtless *want* to believe this, you *could* not do so.

No one could.

Unfortunately, none of the good sense on display here is present in this debate over amnesty—even though the reasoning for the latter is identical to the reasoning of the unfaithful wife.

It is among the most basic obligations of a government to secure its country's borders. As fidelity is essential to preserving the integrity of marriage, so too is border security essential to preserving the integrity of a nation. Indeed, a government that fails to secure its country's borders is unfaithful to its citizens.

Now, according to the Senate Gang of Eight's plan, the government will be expected not only to secure the border, but to see to it that a whole lot of other conditions are satisfied by those who are on "the pathway to citizenship."

There are a few things to note here.

First, if the government either can't or won't fulfill its most basic and simplest of obligations in securing the country's borders now, there is zero reason to accept its assurances that it will fulfill this duty as well as a bunch of new duties later. As my old martial arts instructor used to say, you've got to learn how to walk before you can learn how to run.

With respect to this issue, our government hasn't yet learned how to walk, or even crawl. But the Gang of Eight and their accomplices in the media would have us believe that with the stroke of a pen, the federal government will instantaneously become a marathon runner.

Second, border security is as big of a non-negotiable in governing as fidelity is a non-negotiable in marriage. The citizens of the United States should no more have to negotiate with their government to secure its borders than spouses should have to negotiate with one another to refrain from engaging in adultery. Spouses *owe* it to each other to be faithful. Similarly, the government owes it to its citizens to secure their borders.

However, when Marco Rubio or Chuck Schumer or any other politician favoring amnesty tells us that in order to secure the border we must *first* place millions of illegal immigrants on a "pathway" to citizenship, what they are essentially saying is that *we,* the people's elected representatives, the government, will *not* discharge our constitutional duty *unless* you go along with what *we want.*

Translation: border security most definitely *is* negotiable.

And their accomplices in the media, most tragically the so-called "conservative" media, echo this sentiment.

Finally, when Chuck Schumer, Marco Rubio, and their allies in Washington inform us that our immigration system is "broken," they admit, albeit unwittingly, that *they,* Republicans and Democrats alike, broke it.

Only now, after decades of breaking the system apart piece by piece, they expect for citizens to trust them to construct a new system that is better than ever, a system that will magically solve all of our immigration related issues once and forever.

To take seriously such a claim is to expose oneself as a fool. To get others to take it seriously is to expose oneself as a liar.

Jack Kerwick

Conservative Talk Radio and Amnesty

Radio talk show host Mike Gallagher is the latest "conservative" media personality to endorse amnesty. Since he revealed his Road to Damascus conversion on this topic a few days ago, Gallagher has been skewered by one-time fans.

Perhaps they should cease the skewering by ceasing to listen to Gallagher—or any other talk radio figure who favors amnesty.

More so than the substance of their position, it is the bad faith and condescension with which these "conservatives" argue for their position that justifies tuning them out.

Those of us who affirm American sovereignty and the rule of law have long recognized that a government that wouldn't lift a finger to prevent millions of immigrants from flooding into the country illegally certainly isn't going to now round up and deport them all. So those who insist that this is the only alternative to amnesty set up what logicians call a false dichotomy—one of the logical fallacies identified many moons ago by Aristotle.

Gallagher and his ilk attribute to their opponents a position that the latter do not hold. Worse, their enemies assign to respecters of the rule of law a position that is a species of wishful thinking, and one that the resisters of amnesty have always *known,* and known *better than anyone,* is wishful thinking.

Those who ache for America to remain a sovereign nation of laws have always maintained that it is primarily through *self-deportation* that the illegal immigration issue can be *mitigated,* though never *solved.*

This brings us to another point.

Pro-amnesty "conservative" personalities and politicians—along with such accomplices as Barack Obama, Janet Napolitano, and La Raza—talk about the need for a "solution" to this problem of our "broken" system. But genuinely conservative (and, for that matter, Christian) thinkers have always known that in life, *there are no solutions.* As Thomas Sowell has said, there are only "tradeoffs."

Amnesty, regardless of how it is packaged, is no more a solution to our problems than is the status quo. It isn't even a more effective response to our situation. However, even if it was, this would not make it a solution, for it will give way to still more problems in the future—like an *increase* in illegal immigration, something that, according to border agents, is happening now as a result of all of the talk of amnesty!

For amnesty's apologists to accuse their opponents of "doing nothing" is more dishonesty, more bad faith, on their part.

First, even if it was true that those who resist amnesty favored letting things be entirely as they are, this is still not a matter of doing nothing. It just could be the case—it undoubtedly *is* the case—that here, the problem is less of a problem than is the proposed "solution."

Second, no one wants for things to remain as they are. Those who resist amnesty want for illegal immigrants to be denied all welfare entitlements, social services, employment opportunities, and voting and driving privileges. This way, they will deport themselves. Also, they want for the government to satisfy its job description and secure the country's borders—an obligation that has never been subject to conditions.

Gallagher and his colleagues obviously believe that their listeners are stupid. Why else would they expect them to believe that although *in the past* the government has not managed to secure the borders and deprive illegal immigrants of all the benefits of citizenship—i.e. enforce its own laws—it *will* do so *now*?

And it is hard not to think that Gallagher and company aren't themselves a bit dense. They won't endorse any bill, they insist, unless it *promises* to secure the border.

Even in the midst of all of these government scandals, and despite all of their "limited government" rhetoric, they are still going to accept the government's "promise" to fulfill its constitutional duty—though it hasn't done this in nearly half-a-century.

On second thought, maybe it *is* the substance of their position favoring amnesty that calls for turning off these "conservative" media personalities—at least until they wise up some.

Immigration Facts & Fictions

Among the huge issues with which our nation has to grapple, that of immigration is as huge as any of them. Yet this has become an increasingly difficult task as fiction has eclipsed fact. So as to make some headway on this score, I seek here to sort out the myths from the truths.

Fiction #1: Immigration is a *normative* concept. The assumption seems to be that all things being equal, immigration is a moral good, something that we *ought* to promote and that only a reprobate could reject. It is this assumption that accounts for why "conservative" critics of amnesty invariably insist that they are all in favor of *legal* immigration. And it is this assumption that underlies the oft-repeated slogan that America is "a nation of immigrants."

Fact: Of course, the truth of the matter is that immigration is as morally-neutral a concept as are the concepts of bleeding and moving. Bleeding and moving, taken by themselves, are neither morally good nor morally bad. The same is the case with immigration. It is circumstances, context, that invest these activities with moral worth.

Fiction #2: America is "a nation of immigrants."

Fact: Those who created America were not "immigrants"; they were *settlers*. There is as much of a difference between a settler of a land and those who emigrate to it as there is a difference between one who founds a company and those who invest in it once the founder takes his company public.

Just as, say, there was no Microsoft to invest in until after Bill Gates founded it, there was no America for anyone to emigrate to until after the English colonists settled it.

Fact: But let's suppose that it is correct that America *is* a so-called nation of immigrants. So what? That America has always been a certain way *in the past* does not mean that it should continue upon that course in the future. Unsurprisingly, in other contexts everyone seems to grasp this principle.

For example, no amnesty enthusiast would endorse the argument that we ought to insure that white Christians remain the dominant demographic group in America because America has always been "a nation of (mostly) white Christians." And no one would contend that because America was originally a nation of lots of white slaveholders that we should see to it that it become so once again.

Fiction #3: Since most of us wouldn't be in America if not for the fact that our ancestors came here, it is incumbent upon us to support immigration now. This reasoning takes the form: "I am the product of immigration. Therefore, I support immigration." People like talk radio and Fox News host Sean Hannity never tire of making this argument.

Fact: To see what a terrible argument it is, consider it in light of another: "I am the product of a one night sexual encounter between two intoxicated strangers. Therefore, I support one night stands between drunken strangers." Even more illustrative of the silliness of this reasoning is this piece of illogic: "I am the product of rape. Hence, I support rape."

In reality, most of us are the offspring of, not immigrants, but Americans. Hannity's grandparents were immigrants, as were my great grandparents. But his parents, like mine, were born and bred in America.

Fiction #4: Since the vast majority of contemporary immigrants are Hispanic, opposition to contemporary immigration policy stems from "racism" toward Hispanics.

Fact: This isn't true, but even if it was, we are once again left asking: And...? The citizenry of a sovereign nation has the right to select for itself that immigration policy that it believes best serves the interests of its country. This policy in turn may be a policy of *no immigration,* or it may be a policy of massive immigration. It may permit only immigrants from Sweden, or only those from Africa. Americans don't owe anyone who isn't already a citizen the rights and duties of American citizenship.

Fact: Current levels of immigration would be just as undesirable as they presently are even if all of our immigrants hailed from Sweden: there are simply too many people that have come to America legally and illegally. However, in truth, most of our immigrants are low skilled workers who hail from largely dysfunctional third world countries.

The out-of-wedlock birthrate among Hispanics exceeds that of American whites *and* blacks.

High school drop-out and gang membership rates are also higher among Hispanics than among whites and blacks.

This judgment isn't rooted in "racism." It *is* rooted in reality.

If we are going to have a productive immigration policy, we need first to speak honestly about immigration.

Rubio and Amnesty

Not so long ago, such conservative movement notables as Rush Limbaugh, Sean Hannity, and many of their colleagues were singing the praises of Florida Senator Marco Rubio. The latter, we have been told, is a rock-ribbed conservative and GOP star who could very well be the next president of the United States.

Doubtless, it is courtesy of the pivotal role that he's played in promoting the amnesty agenda of "the Gang of Eight" that accounts for why the enthusiasm for Rubio among movement celebrities at least appears to have cooled some. Hopefully, appearance here coincides with reality, for Rubio is not now, nor has he ever been, a conservative. His position on immigration is just the latest proof of this.

Yet it isn't just that Rubio has been tenaciously advancing amnesty for millions upon millions of illegal immigrants, though this is bad enough. What's worse is the dishonesty that he's shown in his pursuit of this end.

Rubio features in an ad that is played incessantly in Republican-friendly venues in which he tries to convince his party's base that his amnesty plan is "bold, very conservative, a tough line on immigration." But, observes Jon Feere from the Center for Immigration Studies, given "all the exemptions and waivers" contained in his bill, "it is difficult" to buy this.

Rubio also promises that for the 11 million or so amnestied immigrants, there will be "no federal benefits, no food stamps, no welfare, no Obamacare," and "they [will] have to prove that they're gainfully employed."

Feere's response: "Rubio is simply wrong with these assertions." He explains: "Illegal immigrants are already receiving federal benefits and this bill would do nothing to stop that." Moreover, Rubio's plan "would actually extend greater amounts of benefits to illegal immigrants by giving them legal status."

Rubio claims that his plan deals with the problem of illegal immigration "once and for all," but as Feere points out, the 1986 amnesty on which Reagan signed off also promised to deal with this problem "once and for all." It failed abysmally to deliver. Why think things will be different now?

According to Rubio, his bill does not incite immigrants to come to America illegally. Feere remarks that, evidently, Rubio is not paying any mind to "border officials" who have testified to the contrary before Congress.

Feere cites a *Washington Times* article in which Border Patrol Chief Michael J. Fisher's testimony before the Senate is relayed. Fisher is blunt: "We have seen an increase in attempted entries." The article continues: "He [Fisher] said part of the reason for an increase is that Congress is talking about legalizing illegal immigrants, which is luring more foreigners to try to be in the U.S. when amnesty takes effect."

Rubio's claim that amnesty is not "unfair to the people who have done it the right way" is just as bogus as his other assertions. Feere writes: "The reality is that illegal aliens get to stay in the country the moment they apply for amnesty." As soon as they pass "the simple background check, they receive legal status and nearly all the benefits of citizenship [.]"

Rubio's ad calls for us to "stand" with him in putting an end to "de facto amnesty" while supporting "Conservative Immigration Reform." Feere replies that "Rubio wants to turn the de facto amnesty that we're currently experiencing as a result of non-enforcement of immigration laws into a de jure amnesty for millions of people who do not belong here."

At the same time, Rubio "asks you to 'stand' with him, but he himself is standing with Obama, Napolitano, La Raza, the ACLU, and many other amnesty supporters who cannot be described as 'conservative' in any sense of the word."

Feere does a thorough job of exposing Rubio's comprehensive amnesty plan for the sham that it is. However, just a modicum of common sense is enough to see that Rubio and his accomplices in the Gang of Eight are trying to pull one over on us.

Our government has proven itself to be either incapable of or unwilling to enforce our immigration laws up until this point. Now, after Rubio and company heap new conditions upon the old law books, we're expected to believe that the government will finally do what it has neglected doing for decades.

But if you believe this, then you'll believe that Marco Rubio is a conservative.

Byron York and More GOP Folly on the Hispanic Vote

Even had Republicans won the much coveted Hispanic vote in November, Mitt Romney still would have lost.

Thus declares Byron York while recently writing in the Washington Examiner.

Using a New York Times' calculator devised by Nate Silver, York reports that even if Romney "had been able to make history and attract 50 percent of Hispanic voters," he "still would have been beaten, 283 electoral votes to 255."

And had he "been able to do something absolutely astonishing for a Republican and win 60 percent of the Hispanic vote," he "would have lost by the same margin, 283 electoral votes to 255."

To show just how wide of the mark is the conventional wisdom on the GOP's need for Hispanics, York reveals that even had Romney "been able to reach a mind-blowing 70 percent of the Hispanic vote," he "still would have lost [.]" In such a situation, Romney would have won the popular vote while losing the Electoral College, 270-268.

York informs us that Romney would have had to increase his share of the Hispanic vote from the paltry 27 percent that he actually received to a whopping 73 percent to have won in 2012.

Obviously, York concludes, "Romney, and Republicans, had bigger problems than Hispanic voters."

Indeed. Some of us have known all of this for quite some time. We also have known what York tells us next:

"The most serious" of Republicans' problems "was that Romney was not able to connect with white voters who were so turned off by the campaign that they abandoned the GOP and in many cases stayed away from the polls altogether."

Romney, like McCain before him, failed to resonate with white voters.

And judging from the number of whites who decided to either sit out the election or throw in behind Obama or some third party candidate, this failure to connect was huge.

"Recent reports," York relays, "suggest [that] as many as 5 million white voters simply stayed home on Election Day." What exactly does this mean? Well, if whites "had voted at the same rate [that] they did in 2004, even with the demographic changes since then, Romney would have won."

York adds that "the white vote is so large that an improvement of 4 points…would have won the race for Romney."

Given all of this, York facetiously asks: "So which would have been a more realistic goal for Romney—matching the white turnout from just a few years earlier, or winning 73 percent of Hispanic voters?"

York asserts that if 2012 voting patterns remain constant— "whites voting in lower numbers but about 60 percent for Republicans, blacks and Asians turning out in large numbers and voting 90 percent and 70 percent, respectively, for Democrats"— then "Republicans will have to win an astonishingly high percentage of the Hispanic vote to capture the White House."

York then proceeds to debunk the conventional wisdom among Republican politicians and pundits as the conventional folly that it is. "It is simply not reasonable," he states, "to believe that there is something the GOP can do—pass immigration reform, juice up voter-outreach efforts—that will create that result."

So, what must the GOP do?

The bulk of York's piece has all but spelled out the answer to this question: appeal to the millions of disenchanted whites who feel that their interests have been neglected by both national parties.

Yet even now, and in spite of all that he has written, York still tries to avoid being racially explicit. Instead, he writes of the need for Republicans to reach "the millions of Americans who have seen their standard of living decline over the past decades," those to whom Romney failed to appeal. The next Republican presidential candidate who can do this, he is convinced, will win.

York is to be commended for daring to speak a truth that far too many try at all costs to deny. And he is certainly correct when he concludes his article with the reminder that reaching those millions of Americans who otherwise feel betrayed or ignored by Republicans "would do more than any immigration bill or outreach program ever could."

But neither York nor any other Republican can afford to be afraid to say that it is reaching millions of *white* voters that will guarantee the GOP future electoral victories. Nor should they ignore the fact that these same whites do not live by bread alone.

It isn't just material concerns that motivate them, but the sense, the conviction, that political and cultural elites have silently declared a kind of cold war against them: they are the only group that is not supposed to have legitimate interests.

Until Republicans come to terms with this reality, white voter turn-out will remain low.

And Republicans will remain losers.

Paul Greenberg, Neoconservatism and Amnesty

Paul Greenberg's last article proves what many of us have long known: neoconservatives are leftists by another name.

Greenberg waxes orgasmic over President Obama's decision to grant amnesty to millions of illegal aliens. However, like every other champion of amnesty, he unequivocally denies both that he favors amnesty and that Obama has granted any such thing.

In fact, he enthusiastically seconds Obama's line that "the *real* amnesty" is our current system, a system "that hasn't stopped illegal immigration but just *abandoned* those who managed to sneak across the border, sentencing them to a vague limbo somewhere *beyond the reach of law*, offering them neither justice nor mercy" (italics added).

Greenberg is adamant that such a system is radically incompatible with "the America we know and still want to believe in."

The excessive, but all too predictable, use of bumper sticker sloganeering and emotional appeals aside, Greenberg's argument is shockingly bad.

First things first: Our immigration system is *not* "broken." The chief problem with the system lay in the fact that those who are entrusted with its *enforcement* refuse to discharge their duties. Talk of a "broken system" serves both Republicans and Democrats, for it deflects all responsibility from derelict politicians to some abstract, impersonal entity.

Secondly, Greenberg is no doubt correct that there *are* "good hard working people" who will benefit from Obama's and Greenberg's amnesty. However, judging from the fact that roughly *one-third* of the federal prison population consists of illegal aliens, there is also a fair share of very bad beneficiaries of their "mercy."

Thirdly, the fact remains—even if he and his amnesty-loving ilk prefer that we ignore it—that even these "good" people to whom Greenberg refers are *criminals.* Not only did they violate the law in entering this country; of necessity, they've broken a host of other laws—tax laws, driving laws, etc.—once they arrived here.

Fourthly, Greenberg's and Obama's (and most other Democrats' and Republicans') description of the present situation as "the real amnesty" is profoundly disingenuous for two reasons:

(1) As I said before, there are as many illegal immigrants as there are precisely because the amnesty lovers—those who, for economic, political, and/or racial reasons, wish to throw open the floodgates to Hispanics and others from the Third World—have adamantly refused to enforce America's immigration laws.

(2) If we have a de facto amnesty because illegal aliens are "in

the shadows," then we have a de facto amnesty vis-à-vis drug users and drug dealers, rapists, murderers, child molesters, and every other sort of criminal.

If a de facto amnesty regarding illegal immigrants is intolerable, something that needs to be rectified by *legalizing* them, then, presumably, a de facto amnesty concerning all other criminals is intolerable and should be solved by legalizing *them*.

Finally, like all supporters of amnesty, Greenberg insists that no amnesty has taken place, for there are various "standards" that illegal immigrants must meet before their status can change.

The world is ridden with bad ideas, but I can't think of any that more unequivocally convicts its holder of either scandalous gullibility or blatant dishonesty than this one.

Think about it: the government can't fulfill its most basic Constitutional obligation by preventing millions of people from entering the country, but now that they're here, it expects us to believe that it *will* be able to make them comply with a bewildering battery of other laws! This is like a lame person who, while admitting that he can't walk, assures you that if you just give him the chance, he will become a marathon runner.

Also, if these illegal immigrants who are all "good hard working people" deserve "justice and mercy," then isn't it unjust and unmerciful to impose *any* standards at all upon them?

There is one last point that shouldn't be lost upon us: Greenberg argues his case—and that of Obama's—by way of the doctrine of "American Exceptionalism" (AE).

Obama's speech last Thursday night, he says, "was...a tribute to American exceptionalism, for this is a nation bound together not like others, by blood or class or party, but by shared belief and hope [.]"

To be sure, AE is a quintessential egalitarian doctrine. And like all such doctrines, it denies the variety of human existence by reducing human beings to a bunch of interchangeable rights-bearers. This is why it is ready made for leftist ideologues of both the neoconservative and the more recognizable varieties, universalists who want to remake the country—and the world—in the image of their ideology.

After all, when ethnic, racial, religious, and every other kind of consideration that has ever distinguished people from one another are treated as if they don't really exist, then the human species is regarded as a blank slate upon which the champions of Equality can scribble out their fantasies—fantasies like Democracy, say.

The prevailing vision of immigration policy shared by neoconservatives, like Greenberg, and other leftists, like Obama, reflects this same bloodless, lifeless, egalitarianism.

Trump Is Right on Immigration

At the moment, Donald Trump, deservedly, is all of the rage for remarks he made regarding Mexican immigrants to the United States:

> *When Mexico sends its people, they're not sending their best...They're sending people that have lots of problems, and they're bringing those problems with us. They're bringing drugs. They're bringing crime. They're rapists. And some, I assume, are good people.*

Democrats and Republicans, both politicians and their apologists in the "mainstream" and "conservative" media, wasted no time in pouncing upon Trump.

Some thoughts:

First, it is obvious to those with a modicum of intelligence and honesty that Trump never intended to suggest that *all* Mexican immigrants are reprobates. For starters, Trump himself *qualified* his statement by including "good people" among Mexican immigrants. But even if he hadn't done so, it is either bad faith or intellectual density that could lead anyone to confuse a *general* remark of the sort that Trump made with a *categorical* one.

If I say that men are physically stronger than women, do I risk being accused of "sexism" lest I explicitly acknowledge that there are *exceptions?*

Not coincidentally, I'm sure, the indignant who now judge Trump by this standard have been exempting themselves from it for as long as *they* have been condemning *whites* for slavery, Jim Crow, and so forth. Notice: Even though the overwhelming majority of white Americans never owned a slave, and even though there were no fewer than *4,000* black slave *owners* in the antebellum South, talk of historical injustices suffered by "blacks" at the hands of "whites" is *never, ever* fine-tuned by modifiers like "not all," "some," "most," etc.

When Jeb Bush says that immigrants who enter America illegally do so out of "love," no one complains that he "paints with too broad of a brush."

This leads us to our next point.

Second, both those Hispanic "leaders" (read: racialist lobbyists) who are now demanding that GOP presidential contenders distance themselves from Trump as well as those among the latter who are all too eager to comply have hurled themselves onto the horns of a dilemma.

On the one hand, since Trump never implied that *all* Mexican immigrants are criminals, drug dealers, and rapists, his critics must object to his assertion that there are *some* criminals, drug dealers, and rapists coming to America from Mexico.

But if this is their grievance, then they have before them the impossible task of defending a position—there is *no* criminal element among Mexican immigrants—that is *demonstrably, patently* false.

On the other hand, if this is *not* their view; if they concede that there are criminals among Mexican immigrants and that some of them are among the worst of the worst, then they acknowledge that Trump spoke truthfully and, hence, have no *intellectual* or *factual* basis for being upset with him.

That they remain upset with him proves that their motivations are *political* or *ideological.*

Third, that immigrants from Mexico (and other Central and South American countries) are indeed bringing "lots of problems" with them is undeniably *true.* That some of them are "bringing drugs;" that some of them are bringing other sorts of "crime;" and that some of them are "rapists," is *true.*

Fourth, the 19th century philosopher Friedrich Neitzsche memorably remarked that the truth is "hard." For our politicians, partisan media pundits, Hispanic special interest/activist groups, the Immigrant Lobby, the Chamber of Commerce, and the agents of the Racism-Industrial-Complex generally, certain truths about the relentless wave of Third World immigration that's descended upon America for the last 50 years or so aren't just *hard.*

They are intolerable.

Thus, it's not enough that Trump's *position* be *repudiated. Trump* must be *demonized.*

Fifth, that some of Trump's staunchest critics are fellow Republicans speaks volumes—*about his critics.*

Larry Elder once said that between the GOP and the Democrats, there was hardly a dime's worth of difference. If the issue of immigration is a barometer of anything, it's painfully clear that Elder was right on the money.

For years, Republicans, including and especially many of those who have entered the presidential field, have ached every bit as much as their Democratic counterparts for "comprehensive immigration reform"—i.e. *amnesty.* And this aching has endured despite the fact that the last amnesty—presided over by the *Republican*, Ronald Reagan—failed miserably to resolve any problems.

Republicans, like Democrats, have done nothing to secure

the southern border. Even when Republicans controlled the presidency and both houses of Congress, GOP politicians still did nothing to resist the flow of illegal immigration from the south. This, in turn, *encouraged* more of the latter.

Republican governors like Rick Perry and Jeb Bush, presidential candidates who have taken to blasting Trump, along with their colleague, New Jersey Governor Chris Christie, have all arranged for illegal immigrants in their states to avail themselves of in-state tuition rates in the event that they decide to attend college while living illegally in America.

Finally, even assuming, for argument's sake, that it's the case that "immigrants" commit fewer crimes than native born Americans, this is utterly irrelevant to anything that Trump has said.

Immigrants, and illegal immigrants specifically, may be *in* America, but they are not *of* it. An American immigration policy should be designed to benefit *America*. No American benefits from the importation of *any* criminals.

Trump never said that Mexican gutter snipes in America are overrepresented or not among America's gutter snipes. He simply pointed out that there *are* gutter snipes coming to our country from Mexico.

Again, if his opponents believe that this empirically verifiable statement is inaccurate, they should say so. And if they don't object to its truth, then they have no intellectual ground on which to object.

As for their political motivations…well, that's a different story.

ACADEMIA

HIGHER EDUCATION TODAY all too frequently amounts to no education. Rather, academics from institutions small and large; private, public, and religious; community colleges and research universities, tend to be more interested in betraying their vocational calling to educate students in favor of training them in the political ideology of the moment. Consequently, the liberal arts, which have traditionally served the end of liberating the mind and heart, have been subverted, "politicized."

Today, the prevailing ideology is what we usually refer to as "Political Correctness." It is a variant of leftism that tends to assume a largely adversarial stance toward the intellectual, spiritual, and ethical traditions of Western civilization. The articles in this chapter reveal the corrosive effects of the infusion of ideology into higher education, including and especially the extent to which it has impoverished the minds and hearts of students.

Leftist Language-Control on Campus

Recently, the University of New Hampshire's "Bias-Free Language Guide" (BFLG) was revealed to the public. There was a backlash and the President of UNH flew into damage-control mode.

Soon thereafter, administrators decided to pull the guide from its website.

While writing about the BFLG, I assured those readers who may not be in the know that UNH is all too typical of academia today. About as outrageous as the BFLG was President Mark W. Huddleston's assertion that speech "is free and unfettered" on UNH's campus.

The contemporary campus is many things, but a bastion of free and unfettered speech is not one of them.

Take the University of California's program on "Diversity and Faculty development." The program identifies a host of "micro-aggressions." The latter are:

> *the everyday verbal, nonverbal, and environmental slights, snubs, or insults, whether intentional or unintentional, that communicate hostile, derogatory, or negative messages to target persons based solely upon their marginalized group membership.*

A chart is listed with three columns. In the far left column are "themes." In the middle column are "micro-aggression examples." In the far right column are the "messages" that these instances of micro-aggressions convey.

Below is a select list of illustrations:

Because of physical appearances or name, you assume a person to be "foreign-born." By *complimenting* that person on his or her fluency in English—"You speak English very well"—you communicate this message:

"You are not a true American."

If, upon encountering a "person of color" who happens to be good at math, you exclaim, "Wow! How did you become so good in math?" you imply that "people of color are generally not as intelligent as Whites."

It may surprise some people to discover that appeals to "color blindness," at least when they're made by a white person—

or a "White person"—indicates that the person in question "does not want to or need to acknowledge race."

Statements like, "When I look at you, I don't see color;" "There is only one race, the human race;" "America is a melting pot;" and, "I don't believe in race" are offensive. Such statements amount to whites telling non-whites: "Assimilate to the dominant culture."

Those who make these appeals to a color-blind ideal are in effect guilty of "denying the significance of a person of color's racial/ethnic experience and history," of "denying the individual as a racial/cultural being."

Denials of one's "racism," "sexism," and "heterosexism" suffice to convict one of such transgressions.

"I'm not a racist. I have several Black friends" implies that one could "*never* be racist" because of one's circumstances.

"As a woman, I know what you go through as a racial minority" entails that "gender oppression" and "racial oppression" are comparable, or even identical, which in turn erroneously suggests that the woman under discussion could *never* be "racist."

If one asks a racial minority, "Are you sure you were being followed in the store?" one is guilty of "denying the personal experience of individuals who experience bias."

One of my personal favorites on UCLA's list of black balled expressions is what this program refers to as "the *myth* of Meritocracy."

If you say, "I believe the most qualified person should get the job;" "America is the land of opportunity;" "Everyone can succeed in this society if they work hard enough;" or "Men and women have equal opportunities for achievement," then you are culpable of some pretty bad stuff.

If you believe that individuals should be treated according to their merits—not their skin color or gender—then you stand condemned for saying things like: "The playing field is even so if women cannot make it, the problem is with them," and "People of color are lazy and/or incompetent and need to work harder."

According to Walter E. Williams, who also wrote a bit about UCLA's "diversity" instruction, Thomas Sowell referred to these "micro-aggressions" as "micro-totalitarianisms."

Indeed. But lest we get too depressed by the sheer joylessness, the life-draining, the deadly seriousness of these academic totalitarians, we should try having a good laugh at their expense.

I suggest some new items for the folks at UCLA or UNH or any of the Politically Correct storm troopers who are interested.

For starters, these regressive speech codes repeatedly use the language of "women" and "history" (as in "historically marginalized, oppressed," etc."). But doesn't *this* language reinforce and perpetuate Western male "patriarchy" and "misogyny?" After all, etymologically, "woman" literally means "woman-man." That is, the very label of "woman" defines women in terms of their relation to and dependence upon men.

Why not replace "woman" with "estrogen-endowed *bipeds*" or "*homo sapiens?*" ("Human being" and, even worse, "person," are normative or moral concepts. As such, they are "exclusionary," for they exclude non-human animals, fish, insects, and plants. In doing so, the use of "human beings" and "persons" facilitates *speciesism.*)

"History"—I mean "HIS-story"—*genderizes* (academic leftists love making up words) time. It also underscores the traditional Western prejudice that there is a single *objective* reality to which we have access.

There isn't "HIS-story." There are just "*stories*"—and everybody has one.

Since "America" was named after Amerigo Vespucci, a white—or White—explorer, aren't references to "America" and "American" an offense against indigenous peoples and people of color? This being so, "Native American" and "African-American" must go: the former suggests that there was an America before the

Europeans crossed the Atlantic to the Western hemisphere, and the latter is doubly offensive:

Not only is "America" a Eurocentric invention devised to honor a European, so too is "Africa" a name invented by white Europeans—the Romans!

But the greatest chuckle we can get from this self-parody from UCLA is the self-contradiction to be found at the very core of the PC ideology that it embodies.

Assuming for the moment, as this guide assumes, that "racism" is a meaningful notion. If "racism" is immoral, as this guide assumes, then it can only be so if something like a "color-blind" ideal is *accepted*. If it is wrong to treat people differently or badly because of the color of their skin or their cultural background, then this means that we *should* treat people decently *regardless of what they look like* or *where they're from*.

But UCLA regards color-blindness as a function or disguise for "racism."

So it both is and isn't "racist" to treat race as a morally irrelevant characteristic in one's dealings with others.

If we don't laugh, we will cry.

Academia and Diversity

"Diversity" is not just a good in the academic world. It is the *supreme* good, the one good before which all other considerations must yield.

Recently, a colleague expressed a preference for a certain Northeastern city university over a certain Midwestern Christian college because, he said, the former has more "diversity" than the latter.

All that this means, though, is that because this big city university in the Northeast is a racial, ethnic, and socio-economic polyglot and its Midwestern Christian counterpart is just too white, the former is preferable as an educational institution to the latter.

That this god of "diversity" is as educationally invidious as it is false can be seen easily enough.

First, the only diversity that should be of any concern at an institution of higher learning is *intellectual* diversity. "Diversity" of the sort—what we may call "cultural diversity"—that is all too typical at places like that big city university for which my colleague pines, need not and, in fact, *does not* give rise to any more intellectual diversity than can be found at less culturally heterogeneous institutions.

This brings us to the next point: "cultural diversity" not only doesn't correspond to a rise in intellectual diversity; it invariably corresponds to a rise in *political uniformity*. This is crucial, for the promotion of "cultural diversity" is nothing more or less than the promotion of a left-wing ideological agenda.

While academics, like my colleague, look upon predominantly white colleges as insufficiently "diverse," they wouldn't even think to level this same criticism against "historically *black* colleges." They cannot, however, have it both ways: if a predominantly white Christian school is educationally inferior because of *its* mono-racial character, then, *mutatis mutandis*, black schools must also be educationally inferior because of *their* racially homogenous character.

Moreover, for all of their clamoring over the need for greater "diversity," academics don't want things so diverse that politically *incorrect* perspectives are permitted a hearing on campus. Representation of fundamentalist Christians, moral traditionalists, conservatives, libertarians, and anarchists, is not only never in demand; its anathema.

Thirdly, the idea that a predominantly, or even exclusively, white student body somehow militates against a quality education is offensive. But it's offensive only because the history of Western civilization exposes just how patently absurd is the idea that racial homogeneity precludes intellectual richness.

The ideas that have composed the West's consciousness from at least the time of the ancient Greeks and Romans over 2500 years ago through to the present day have derived, overwhelmingly, from white men. It isn't that others haven't made lasting contributions, of course. But even and especially in the eyes of its staunchest *critics,* Western civilization has always been identified with the civilization of *European*—i.e. Caucasian—peoples.

This is fact.

It is equally a fact that it is only either a paralyzing ignorance of reality or incorrigible dishonesty that could prompt anyone to deny with a straight face that the Western tradition is the most intellectually heterogeneous—the most philosophically and theologically *diverse*—tradition in all of human history.

The contemporary academic fiction that Western civilization, by virtue of the "dead white males" that historically shaped it, is somehow an intellectually stagnant monolith is worse than nonsense; to borrow a line from one of those dead white males, the 18th century English philosopher, Jeremy Bentham, it is "nonsense on stilts."

A profound sense of individuality spawned both the passion and daring of those legions of dead white males from throughout the last nearly three millennia to whom we owe our civilization. That "diversity"—or, more accurately, "Diversity"—has become the new deity in, of all places, academia, is among the most sobering, most tragic, of commentaries on our age, for it proves that if the spirit of the Western mind hasn't evaporated, it is beyond the academic world that it is to be found.

Academic Justice, not Freedom, says The Harvard Crimson

Sandra Korn is a Harvard University undergraduate student and a writer for *The Harvard Crimson.* In a recent edition of the school's paper, she argues for abandoning the traditional value of "academic freedom" in favor of what she calls, "academic *justice.*"

Korn may still be only a student, but both the lines along which she thinks as well as the ease with which she articulates her thoughts reveals to all with eyes to see the character of the academic environment in which she's been reared: those who she wishes to deprive of academic freedom are just those academics who refuse to endorse the leftist ideology of Korn and her professors.

Korn singles out as instances of teacher-scholars who should have been stripped of their academic freedom just and only those figures who are noted for their penchant for smashing the sacred cows of the left.

Richard J. Herrnstein is one such example. Herrnstein is probably most distinguished for having co-authored along with Charles Murray the now famous, *The Bell Curve.* However, the thesis that IQ differences vary with race and that, to at least some extent, these differences are genetic, is one that he defended two decades earlier, back in 1971. Because of this position of his, militant student activists disrupted Herrnstein's classes and demanded that, along with sociologist Christopher Jencks (another thought criminal), he be fired.

Quoting Herrnstein, Korn relays that while claiming to have not been "bothered...personally" by the attacks against him, Herrnstein admitted that he was deeply troubled by the fact it was now "hazardous for a professor to teach certain kinds of views" at Harvard. Korn replies that this was *precisely* the point of "the SDS [Students for a Democratic Society] activists—they wanted to make the 'certain kinds of views' they deemed racist and classist unwelcome on Harvard's campus."

Harvey Mansfield is another person upon whom Korn sets her sights. She charges Mansfield with "publishing...sexist commentary under the authority of a Harvard faculty position" and avows that she "would happily organize with other feminists on campus to stop him" from continuing to do so.

Korn admits that while it could very well be the case that student activists are guilty of infringing upon the academic freedom of the Herrnsteins and Mansfields of the world, this "obsession with the doctrine of 'academic freedom' often seems to bump against something [that] I think [is] much more important: 'academic justice.'"

The "obsession" with academic freedom Korn thinks is "misplaced," for "no academic question is ever 'free' from [such] political realities" as "racism, sexism, and heterosexism [.]" After all, since "our university community opposes" such things, "it should ensure that this research…promoting or justifying oppression…does not continue." *This* is in keeping with the demands of "academic justice."

So too does the craving for "academic justice" account for the decision of the American Studies Association at Harvard to boycott "Israeli academic institutions until Israel ends its occupation of Palestine." The ASA, Korn explains, are interested, not in resorting to "the 'freedom' game" of "those on the right," but in achieving "social justice." Thus, they "take the moral upper hand."

Korn concludes by reiterating the central thesis of her essay that our "obsessive reliance on the doctrine of academic freedom" prevents us from considering "more thoughtfully what is just."

In a sane world, a world that hasn't been subverted by decades of leftism, it would be viewed as nothing less than a scandal that any college student, let alone a student at one of the world's most prestigious institutions of higher learning, would hold Korn's views, to say nothing of publishing them.

Traditionally, the university had been regarded as among the premiere *civilizing* institutions, the place where students educated in just those intellectual and moral habits that would enable them to formulate, articulate, and defend their own convictions while treating those of their opponents with respect and even charity.

The academic world inhabited by the Korns of our world is a radically different kind of place. Views with which one disagrees are not to be *refuted*, but *condemned*, and their proponents *demonized*. The university exists not for the sake of acquiring and conveying truth and knowledge, but for the sake of "social justice"—i.e. a totalizing leftist ideology that is to be imposed, "by whichever means necessary," upon both students and faculty alike.

Activism: The Ideal of a Liberal Arts Education

Dinesh D'Souza's latest documentary, *America: Imagine a World without Her,* features interviews with such leftist academic rock stars as Howard Zinn. However, it's crucial for Americans, and particularly those American who are parents, to realize that the contemporary academic world is chock full of lesser known Zinns.

The traditional academic ideal of the disinterested pursuit and dissemination of knowledge has fallen on hard times. Professors in the humanities and social sciences have spent no small portion of the 20th century lambasting it as, at best, incorrigibly naïve. Usually, though, they've gone further, rejecting the traditional ideal as a noxious, indeed, an *oppressive,* fiction.

In its stead, academics have replaced it with a new ideal, one more suited to their own ideological agenda: the purpose of academia, it is now widely held, is to promote the pursuit of *"social justice."*

In other words, a "liberal arts education" should have as its aim the production of, *not* "well rounded" individuals, as had been traditionally thought, but *social activists*—i.e. committed leftists.

A more disastrous turn of events couldn't have been imagined for academia.

For centuries, it was recognized that the academic world's contribution to the preservation and enrichment of Western civilization lay precisely in the fact that, unlike most of our activities, *its* activities were most decidedly not *utilitarian* or *practical.* Vocational schools, for example, are utilitarian in that students are *trained* for the sake of accomplishing some predetermined *goal:* mastery in one's vocation and the monetary benefits that are expected to accrue from this.

College and university students, in stark contrast, are supposed to receive, not training, but an *education.* This education, in turn, is no more oriented toward some goal over and above itself than is friendship so oriented. The education is *its own reward*: learning for learning's sake—not the sake of money, fame, fortune, or any other extrinsic goal.

Given this vision of academia, even the traditional ideal of the disinterested *pursuit* of *truth* is problematic, for it suggests that the raison d' entre of university learning is some transcendent purpose—the acquisitions of knowledge—that can be attained only *after* students acquire an encyclopedic collection of "facts" or "propositions."

But if the traditional ideal is problematic, the activist ideal is ruinous. It isn't just that, in its current manifestation, the latter is enlisted in the service of a *leftist* political agenda. The primary problem is that it promotes a *political* agenda of any sort.

The activist ideal transforms academia into a political institution. Education is now "politicized," as we say, but say confusingly, for a "politicized education" is a contradiction in terms. *Education* has been jettisoned in favor of *training.* Only the training in question is not training in a vocation, but in an *ideology,* and in the methods and ways by which this ideology can be spread to the four corners of the Earth.

"Education" has now been rendered a thoroughly *practical* or *utilitarian* matter like any other political endeavor.

This being so, it promises to cultivate in students intellectual and moral habits that are anything but virtues.

The political activist is forever focused on *the future.* The past—specifically the past of Western civilization—is treated as a history of unmitigated oppression. The present is considered to be either an impediment to a brighter tomorrow or the means by which the promised land of the activist's imaginings will be brought to fruition.

But it is from exactly *this* temporal orientation—this future-centered vision—that a liberal arts education is meant to *emancipate* students.

For one, a training in social activism renders students ignorant of their inheritance by essentially severing them from their past and immunizing them against delighting in the nuances of the present.

That is, when it isn't tempered with an understanding of the past and an appreciation for the present—a knowledge of its location in the time continuum—this eagerness for the future embodies a shallowness that impoverishes the imagination.

This in turn breeds arrogance—an invincible arrogance—insofar as it nourishes the belief that humanity's liberation from the darkness in which it remains mired will only be achieved once this present generation drags the rest of us—kicking and screaming, if need be—to our salvation.

And this brings us to another critical point: Because every utopia requires for its realization an activist *government,* the activist ideal encourages in students a partiality toward coercion over persuasion, a disposition—no, a *determination*—to use *force* rather than engage in *dialogue.*

Simply put, the activist ideal inculcates *bellicosity.*

D'Souza's film features footage in which Howard Zinn unabashedly declares that his scholarship and teaching is driven by a desire to *change the world.* In doing so, he expresses the activist ideal of the contemporary academy.

Unfortunately, the ideal is bad for academia and bad for the world.

Envy No Vice for Academics

If more of the American electorate were aware of three things, I would like to think that one of our two national parties would have a significantly more difficult time maintaining power.

These three things pertain to the contemporary American university.

And the party that has an interest invested in keeping Americans in the dark about these facts is the party of which President Barack H. Obama is the titular head.

The first fact is that the professorial class consists overwhelmingly of hard leftists.

The second is that these hard leftists vote almost invariably for Democrats and never—never—for Republicans.

Third and finally, Democratic politicians are continually busy at work advocating on behalf of the ideas that their academic counterparts are just as busily formulating. To put it more simply, there is an inseparable connection between the theoretical imaginings of leftist academics and the policy prescriptions of leftist politicians—i.e. Democrats.

Take the Democrats tactic of choice, for instance.

Democrats are known for nothing if not their penchant for wailing over "the greed" of "millionaires and billionaires" who "exploit" the rest of us by refusing to "pay their fair share" of taxes. As his relentless assaults against his election opponent have amply demonstrated, Barack Obama is the Democrat *par excellence* when it comes to advancing this line.

Republicans refer to this as the politics of "class warfare" and/or "envy." Democrats resist the charge.

However, when we look beyond the surface of sound bites, sloganeering, and photo shoots to the university, what we discover is that the Republicans' charge is not wide of the mark. Leftists, you see—always to be counted upon to depart from the ethical traditions of the civilization to which they owe their existence—do not regard envy as the vicious character disposition that it has always been held to be.

Much less do they view envy as one of the seven deadly sins that St. Thomas Aquinas and other Christian theorists spent centuries deploring.

Ronald Dworkin is one of the better known legal scholars of our time. A Harvard professor and prolific writer on topics ranging from philosophy of law to ethics to political philosophy, he has engaged in lively exchanges with the most distinguished of contemporary thinkers, including Supreme Court Justice Antonin Scalia.

In other words, Dworkin is not some fringe thinker.

This is important to bear in mind, for Dworkin reveals just how Obama and his fellow partisans think about "social" or "economic justice."

For Dworkin, justice is to be measured in terms of an "ideal" distribution of resources. There are two kinds of resources, "personal" and "impersonal." The former consists in those mental and physical attributes, like health, strength, talent, that make success in life either harder or easier to come by. Impersonal resources, on the other hand, are material goods, tangible things—properties and property rights.

We can determine whether there exists an ideal distribution of resources—justice—by applying what Dworkin refers to as "the *envy* test." He writes: "Someone envies the resource-set of another person when he would prefer that resource-set to his own, and would therefore trade his own for it." If, though, "no member of the community envies the total set of resources under the control of any other member," then "equality is perfect" and, thus, justice is achieved.

Notice, an "ideal" distribution of resources is an "equal" distribution of resources, and such a distribution is a "just" distribution.

Things get worse.

Dworkin invites us to engage in an imaginary "auction" where only impersonal resources can be traded. That is, only property and property rights can be "equalized." Still, even if there is a perfect equality of material possessions, some people may still envy the looks and talents of others. And even if personal resources are more or less comparable, luck may supply unfair advantages to some people.

In order to rectify, as much as possible, these situations, there must be "compensatory strategies to repair…inequalities in personal resources and luck." These "compensatory programs" can be "modeled on hypothetical insurance markets" and "financed by general taxation."

Dworkin is clear that if there are conflicts between the demands of equality and liberty, then "invasions of liberties" will be justified if they are "necessary to protect an egalitarian distribution of resources and opportunities."

The point here is clear: there is *nothing* of a person's that the government may not confiscate as long as there are others in society who envy it.

The kind of thinking on display in the work of academics like Ronald Dworkin finds expression in the policies of Democratic politicians like Barack Obama.

This is what Americans need to realize—even if the Democrats would like for us to remain ignorant of it.

The Creed: Academia's Monologue

On June 6, Richard Cravatts' article, "No Free Speech for Exposers of Campus Anti-Semitism" was published at Front Page Magazine.

Cravatts relays the challenges of Tammi Rossman-Benjamin. The latter is "a lecturer at UC [University of California] Santa Cruz and co-founder of the AMCHA Initiative, an organization that investigates, documents, educates about, and combats anti-

Semitism at institutions of higher education in the U.S."

More specifically, Rossman-Benjamin has been waging a campaign against what she describes as "an advanced anti-Israel and pro-Palestinian discourse" that has managed to exclude all alternative narratives.

As a result, untold numbers of California college students have been brainwashed into believing the worst about Israel while her defenders, particularly her Jewish defenders, have been forced to endure a hostile environment.

The university should be a hostile environment for neither students nor their instructors—regardless of whether they are Jewish or non-Jewish, and regardless of the issue. But it will surprise none of its observers, and surprise even less those of us who inhabit it, that Israel is not well regarded in the contemporary university. In fact, whether or not Israel is ever mentioned is neither here nor there: to know the university is to know that she promises to be despised.

That there is "an advanced anti-Israel and pro-Palestinian discourse" that has "dominated" the University of California is due to the fact that it is but another variation of a much larger but equally advanced anti-Western discourse that has dominated institutions of higher learning everywhere for decades.

Interestingly, for as sophisticated as the members of the professorial class are thought to be, the framework within which they ply their respective disciplines in the liberal arts and humanities is simple to the point of being simplistic.

Actually, it is grossly simplistic.

From the standpoint of this framework, the cosmos consists of two, and *only* two, types of beings: Oppressors and the Oppressed. Moreover, there are no individuals, but only collectives, abstract categories defined in terms of race, gender, sexual orientation, religion, socio-economic class, and region.

This worldview I have elsewhere referred to as "the Creed." Anyone who spends any amount of time, whether as a student or as an instructor, will soon come to know the Creed well enough.

According to the Creed, the white, Western, Christian, heterosexual man (or "male") is the universe's villain extraordinaire. All others are the victims of his predatory machinations.

Of course, within this scheme there are further gradations. The medieval thinkers subscribed to what has been called "the Great Chain of Being." At the apex of the chain is the greatest of beings, God. Angels and, then, humans, rank lower. Beneath them are animals, then plants. But at the bottom of the scale is the worst of beings: Satan.

The idea here is that the greater the being, the better kind of being it is. Conversely, the less being something has, the worse it is.

The Creed involves something similar. Only here it is the white, Western, Christian, heterosexual male that occupies something like the position that Satan occupies in the Great Chain of Being. At the same time, women and non-whites rank higher along the scale. Still, while white women and white homosexual men are perennial victims of sexism and homophobia, respectively, they nevertheless occupy lower rungs in the ladder than do non-whites of both genders and all sexual orientations, for in addition to being subjected to these evils, non-whites are also prey to racism—and there is nothing more egregious than racism.

The anti-Israel/pro-Palestinian narrative against which Rossman-Benjamin rails fits seamlessly into the Creed. Judaism, though having originated in the East, has been integral to Western civilization. And Israel, with its economic, cultural, and military might, is *the* outpost of Western civilization in the Islamic world.

Palestinians, in stark contrast, have none of the affluence or power of their Israeli rivals. They are also non-Western, Muslim, and, for the most part, non-white. Their conflict with Israelis emblematizes for guardians of the Creed the perpetual contest that it identifies as the essence of life, the struggle between

Oppressor and Oppressed.

The Creed is the orthodoxy of the contemporary academy. Unfortunately for Tammi Rossman-Benjamin, she is not likely to succeed in undermining the "anti-Israel and pro-Palestine discourse" that has "dominated" the university until she first defeats the Creed that it expresses.

Occupying the White Male Syllabus at Berkeley

Upon witnessing the trials of Nazi war criminals in Jerusalem, Hannah Arendt remarked that they shared in common one salient feature: "it was not stupidity," she said, "but a curious, quite authentic inability to think." This inability or refusal to think is on full display in a student editorial—"Occupy the Syllabus"—that was recently published by *The Daily Californian.*

Berkeley students Rodrigo Kazuo and Meg Perret "call" for an "occupation of syllabi" that was "instigated" by their experience in "an upper-division course in classical social theory." The syllabus for this course is scandalous, for it "employed a standardized canon of theory that began with Plato and Aristotle, then jumped to modern philosophers: Hobbes, Locke, Hegel, Marx, Weber and Foucault, all of whom are white men." Not "a single woman or person of color" was included.

These white theorists can't relate to "the lives of marginalized peoples," or "gender or racial oppression." In fact, they didn't "even engage with the enduring legacies of European colonial expansion, the enslavement of black people and the genocide of indigenous peoples in the Americas." When "race and gender" *are* mentioned in "the white male canon," they "are at best incomplete and at worst racist and sexist."

The student writers allege that "the classroom environment felt so hostile to women, people of color, queer folks and other marginalized subjects that it was difficult for us to focus on course material." Even worse, there were times "when we felt so uncomfortable that we had to leave the classroom in the middle of a lecture."

The white male canon is a "tyranny," Kazuo and Perret conclude, that students must "dismantle [.]" In its place, they must "demand the inclusion of women, people of color and LGBTQ* [Lesbian, Gay, Bisexual, Transgendered, Queer] authors on our curricula."

What a pity. These poor students, like the vast majority of their peers in liberal arts departments around the country, have indeed been getting the shaft. But this is because they are not receiving an *education* at all; rather, it is *training,* or maybe *indoctrination,* in an ideology, a doctrine or creed, of which they are the *unfortunate* recipients.

It is obvious, so *painfully* obvious, that these Berkeley students are paralyzed by "the inability to think" to which Arendt alludes. Their essay amounts to a *caricature* of the Politically Correct orthodoxy, i.e. the militant leftist ideology, for which academia has become known—and for which it is routinely ridiculed. In an essay that can't be more than a 1,000 words, there is scarcely a leftist stock phrase, cliché, or sacred cow that isn't exploited.

The problem, though, is not that the students are incapable of thinking beyond *leftist* stock phrases and clichés; the problem is that they are incapable of thinking beyond *stock phrases* and *clichés.* As Arendt writes:

> *Clichés, stock phrases, adherence to conventional, standardized codes of expression and conduct have the socially recognized function of protecting us against reality, that is, against the claim on our thinking attention which all events and facts arouse by virtue of their existence.*

Arendt admits that if "we were responsive to this claim [on our thinking attention] all of the time, we would soon be exhausted [.]" In other words, we must trade, at least much of the time, in "standardized codes of expression and conduct [.]" However, "the difference" between some of us and the average Nazi defendant that she observed is that the latter "clearly knew of no such claim" on *his* "thinking attention."

And what was true in Eichmann seems equally true of these Berkeley students.

The latter can also be likened to some of Socrates' pupils to whom Arendt refers, men who were not "content being taught how to think without being taught a *doctrine*," a creed on which to hang their hats (italics added). Yet the activity of thinking "is equally dangerous to *all creeds* and, by itself, does not bring forth any new creed" (italics added).

Substantively, of course, Kazuo's and Perret's comments are outrageous. The point here, though, is that *even if* there was truth to them, that they are framed in terms of all of the buzzwords of *any* orthodoxy—in this case, the prevailing orthodoxy at Berkeley and in academia generally—reveals the shallowness of their intellects.

Moreover, Kazuo's and Perret's op-ed serves as an *indictment* of the faculty and administrators of their institution. Not only has Berkeley (like colleges and universities throughout the land) failed miserably to supply their students (in the liberal arts) with an education, the ability and willingness to interrogate their own most cherished doctrines. Berkeley has actually *supplied* them with *the doctrine* that resulted in this essay: After all, can anyone really doubt that Kazuo and Perret *are,* from tip to tail, the children of Berkeley?

What's ironic—*richly* ironic—is that it is largely their *white male* instructors that filled their heads with this conceptual claptrap in the first place.

Rather than occupying their instructors' syllabi, the Kazuos and Perrets of the world would be much better served trying, for once, to occupy their own minds instead of allowing them to be fed with the dogmas and vapid slogans of their professors.

Brown University and Ray Kelly: An Eye into the Academic World

In October of 2103, New York Police Commissioner Ray Kelly arrived at the prestigious Brown University to deliver a speech.

It never happened. Student protesters, determined to silence Kelly, shouted him down.

In an attempt to abate the hostility of his audience, Kelly is said to have remarked: "I thought this was the Academy...where we're supposed to have free speech." A Brown administrator on the scene also expressed incredulity regarding the "inability" of these Brown students'—self-avowed "social justice activists" to a man and woman—"to have a dialogue[.]"

Jenny Li, the (Brown) student who organized the anti-Kelly demonstration, explained that in advance of Kelly's appearance, she and other students petitioned the university to cancel the event. However, when administrators refused to accommodate them, Li and her fellow activists "decided to cancel it for them." Their victory in doing so, Li adds, is "a powerful demonstration of free speech."

Christina Paxson, President of Brown, expressed her "deepest regret" to Commissioner Kelly and assured everyone that the protesters' conduct is at once "indefensible" and "an affront both to civil democratic society and to the university's core values and the free exchange of views."

To date the disrupters have not faced any disciplinary action.

The significance of this episode has little to do with its specifics and everything to do with the fact that it supplies us with a microcosmic perspective on *the contemporary university*.

First of all, *no one*, much less an eminently sensible man like Ray Kelly and seasoned academics like the aforementioned Brown administrators, can possibly believe that the contemporary Academy is an oasis of "free speech" and open-ended dialogue.

In fact, as anyone who's spent any amount of time there knows all too well, the university is much more like a *puddle* of free speech and dialogue than an oasis. In fact, it is more akin to a desert in this regard.

While the incident in question admittedly involves *students,* the latter are simply marching to the beat of the drums of the faculty and administration, not just of Brown, but of colleges and universities throughout the country. They at once reflect and reinforce an academic *culture* that has been at least a half-of-a-century in the making.

It is as tragic as it is scandalous—and let there be no mistakes about it, this *is* one of the great scandals of our age—that there is far *less* individuality and "free speech" in our country's liberal arts and humanities departments than can be found among any random collection of construction workers or plumbers.

While there *are* exceptions (yours truly is a case in point), the overwhelming majority of academics in the liberal arts are left-wing ideologues. This is no criticism—just a brute fact.

There is indeed a prevailing ideology, an *orthodoxy,* really, that draws the lines of acceptable discourse. For lack of a better name, we can call this orthodoxy "Political Correctness," for it is the same orthodoxy that has long drawn the lines of acceptable discourse in the popular culture.

The only difference is that non-academics, like construction workers and plumbers, say, have the daring and imaginativeness to transgress the orthodoxy's boundaries. Academics, in contrast, seek to *strengthen* these strictures on speech.

In other words, the relationship between the academic and his society has been radically subverted. Worse, the lion's share of the blame for this subversion rests upon his (or her) shoulders.

There is another point that can't be lost upon us.

Traditionally, a liberal arts education was intended to render students preeminently *civil* by making them into articulate, knowledgeable conversationalists capable of both drawing upon the inheritance of their civilization—Western civilization—as well as enriching it. It was an education that required great humility from those who would undertake it, for the present generation, it was understood, was just one voice in this millennia-old conversation linking the past with the present and future.

The attitude on display at Brown and exemplified by Jennifer Li is not only entirely incompatible with a traditional liberal arts education; the former and the latter are mutually antithetical. There are two reasons for this.

For one, today's students, like their teachers, are generally contemptuous toward the past. The past is viewed as a "dark age" ridden with "white racism," "sexism," "homophobia," "speciesism," "xenophobia," etc. The present bequeathed to us by our past, as Barack Obama memorably remarked, is something the needs to be "fundamentally transformed"—i.e. *destroyed.*

As for future generations, while lip service is routinely paid to them, it is not difficult to show that if the interests of unborn human beings threaten to impede present designs, then they too must be marginalized.

Secondly, academics and the student activists who they are busy creating are *angry.* And they spare no occasion to express that anger.

Since at least the time of the 1960's the expression of anger has been treated as tantamount to the expression of *authenticity.* However, since no one cares to try to reason with an angry person—regardless of how authentic he may fancy himself to be—about any topic, much less controversial topics, conversation is impossible with the perpetually angry.

And so too is a genuine liberal arts education impossible as long as pride and anger are the emotions that the academy insists upon fostering.

St. Louis University: Rewriting History in Catholic Higher Education

St. Louis University, a Roman Catholic institution of "higher learning," capitulated to student and faculty demands to remove a 19th century statue from campus.

The statue, which commemorates the missionary efforts of Jesuit priest, Pierre-Jean De Smet, depicts the latter on an elevated platform holding a cross over the heads of two American Indians.

The school paper, *The University News,* featured an editorial by SLU student, Ryan McKinley. According to McKinley, the statue deserves to be removed from campus because it reflects "a history of colonialism, imperialism, racism and of Christian and white supremacy."

Ironically, it's a shame that this event gained national news coverage, for in doing so, the public risks receiving the impression that there is something unusual afoot at SLU. However, the tragic truth of the matter is that the anti-Western ideology—and, hence, the anti-white, anti-Christian, anti-American, anti-male ideology—underwriting the fuss over the De Smet statue is *the* conceptual lens of the whole academic world.

But it's even worse than this: the ideology on display at SLU transcends academia, for it is *the* Zeitgeist of contemporary Western and American culture.

What all of this in turn means is that academics are guilty on three scores.

First, they stand convicted of preaching an ideology—*any* ideology—while they should have been teaching.

Secondly, in advancing the anti-Western ideology that is our culture's dominant worldview, academics are guilty of promoting an especially *pernicious* ideology.

Thirdly—and this is the most egregious of the crimes for which they stand condemned—academics are guilty of promoting an ideology that *is* their culture's *dominant worldview*, i.e. the status quo.

When Hannah Arendt observed the trials of Nazi war criminals, she claimed to have been struck by "the curious, but quite authentic, inability" on their part "to think." It is this phenomenon, Arendt noted, and not any especially wicked motives, that accounted for the Holocaust. Neither Adolph Eichmann nor any of his partners in crime were inclined to think beyond their stock of conventional phrases and clichés. This inability or unwillingness to think critically is inseparable from, if it isn't identical with, an inability or unwillingness to exercise *self-rule* or *autonomy*: the defendants were only interested in *obeying* others.

Of course, Arendt knew that there was nothing unique about the Nazis in this regard. *Most* people much the time and *all* people some of the time succumb to the temptation to relinquish critical thought. After all, it is far easier to go along in order to get along. It requires no courage, no mental exertions, to *conform* to prevailing opinion, to "obey."

Yet this inability to think—to obey The Majority—has given rise to the worst sorts of evils.

It is this inclination toward mental conformity that accounts for the readiness with which otherwise reasonable, intelligent people imbibe the ideology of the students and faculty at St. Louis University. It is this inclination that explains the seeming inability of such folks to think or speak beyond the ideology's stock terms.

"Colonialism;" "imperialism;" "racism;" "white supremacy;" "Christian supremacy"—these are the soundbites, the talking points, the bumper sticker slogans, that define both the substance and the boundaries of the PC Zeitgeist.

A Taoist scholar once wrote that every "ism" is a "wasm." His point is that once a current of thought has been abstracted from its place in the complex of mental activities and frozen as a doctrine, an "ism," it has been divested of the dynamic character, the nuances and open-endedness that originally made it a living belief. The dogma that replaces it is necessarily an oversimplification, a caricature.

It's of no surprise that our student and faculty activists at SLU (and everywhere else) *must* think in terms of "isms."

Yet, as I mentioned, students don't start learning about the "isms" once they get to the university. Regrettably, the ideology that their professors reinforce in the college classroom is the same ideology on which their minds have been fed by the larger culture all of their lives.

From their first day in college, students are disposed to acquiesce in the ideology with which their professors will besiege them for the next four (or more) years. So, rather than inculcate in students those intellectual virtues—curiosity, daring, discernment, and excitement—necessary for *challenging* the prejudices that they've inherited from the larger society, faculty *strengthen* those prejudices.

In doing so, faculty strengthen their students' "curious, but quite authentic inability to think."

But in burdening them with this handicap, the self-same professors who ache to make their students into little saviors of the world actually frustrate the pursuit of their own goal, for, as Arendt observed, the inability or unwillingness to think—to cultivate *individuality*—all too often translates into the ability and willingness to aid and abet evil.

Edmund Burke famously said that the only thing that is necessary for evil to triumph is for good men to do nothing. He was right. However, there are plenty of reasonably decent people that may not be aware that evil is in their midst if they lack the ability, or the willingness, to genuinely, thoroughly, *think* about the ideas that "everyone" accepts as true.

As for those who dare to think, they don't have their college professors to thank for it.

The University of New Hampshire's Bias-Free Language Guide: More Thought Control in Academia

If there remained any doubts that academia is among the most thoughtless places in the cosmos, the University of New Hampshire just put them to rest once and for all.

The breathtaking Political Correctness embodied by UNH's recently released, "Bias-Free Language Guide" (BFLG), proves that higher education has become a one-dimensional caricature of itself. Indeed, right-wing reactionaries couldn't have done a better job in calling attention to the intellectual and moral shallowness, the remarkable lack of seriousness—or is it the remarkable abundance of *deadly* seriousness?—of academia.

And before anyone objects that the entire academic establishment shouldn't be judged on the basis of the actions of one school, it should be borne in mind that the *zeitgeist* expressed by UNH's latest de facto speech code *is* one and the same left-wing orthodoxy that has long achieved a stranglehold over the university.

The BFLG "is meant to serve as a starting point" in rethinking "terms related to age, race, class, ethnicity, nationality, gender, ability, sexual orientation and more" for the purpose of promoting "inclusive excellence in our campus community." In short, words that are infected with "bias" are "problematic" or "outdated;" those that are alleged to be "bias-free" are "preferred."

"People of advanced age" and "old people" are preferred. Terms like "older people," "elders," "seniors," and "senior citizen" are problematic and outdated.

Yes, believe it or not, "'old people' has been reclaimed by some older activists who believe the standard wording of old people lacks the stigma of the term 'advanced age.'" Moreover, the term "old people" also halts "the euphemizing of age." The latter is bad because in "euphemizing," we assume that "age is a negative."

"Poor person" and "person from the ghetto" are problematic and outdated. In contrast, "person who lacks advantages that others have" and "low economic status related to a person's education, occupation and income" are preferable.

Wow. If "poor person" is now a Politically Incorrect term, then it would appear that no word is safe.

Indeed: Even use of the word "homeless" reflects insensitivity on the part of the user. The BFLG explains that "homeless" "reduces the person to being defined by their housing rather than as a person first [.]"

Instead, "homeless" should give way to "person-experiencing homelessness."

"Obese" and "overweight" are offensive descriptors: the former is "the medicalization of size" while the latter is "arbitrary." Even "fat" is on its way to being preferable to either of these terms, for some "people of size"—the preferred term of choice—and "their allies" have "reclaimed" it.

"Non-disabled" is preferred to "able-bodied" and "normal."

"Person who is blind/visually impaired" is preferable to "blind person."

"U.S. citizen" or "resident of the U.S." is preferable to "American," for the latter "usually...fails to recognize South America."

"Foreigners" should be rejected in favor of "international people."

"Illegal alien" and "illegal" fail to affirm the humanity of those in question. But even "undocumented immigrant or worker," though generally preferable to the alternative, isn't wholly successful in recognizing "the person's humanity first."

"Sexual preference" is bad because it suggest that "being gay or lesbian is voluntary and therefore 'curable.'" On the other hand, "sexual orientation" and "sexual identity" are good.

"Homosexual" is out; "gay, lesbian, same gender-loving

(SGL)" is in.

Alternative "lifestyle" is unacceptable in that it has been "used by anti-gay extremists to denigrate lesbian, gay, bisexual and transgender lives." "LGBTQ" is the only appropriate term here.

"Parenting" and "nurturing" are "non-gendered" activities. Thus, only if "gender is specifically implied" is it permissible to use the otherwise problematic terms of "mothering" and "fathering."

"Opposite sex" is offensive and insensitive. "*Other* sex" is more inclusive.

These are just *some* of the revisions to our language that the BFLG suggests. It also identifies a number of "micro-aggressions" like the "micro-assault," the "micro-insult," and the "micro-invalidation." A micro-assault is what the guide refers to as a "verbal attack." The example used is that of one person who, upon encountering another "using a mobile chair for long distance travel," questions the latter about his or her ability to walk.

This is a micro-assault.

A micro-insult is "a form of verbal or silent demeaning through insensitive comments or behavior," and a micro-invalidation consists in "degrading a person's wholeness through making false assumptions about the other's ability, causing a sense of invalidation."

UNH President, Mark W. Huddleston, insists that the BFLG is not school policy. He also claims to be "troubled by many of the things in the language guide, especially the suggestion that the use of the term 'American' is misplace or offensive."

Whether Huddleston is sincere on this score, or whether he realized that the language guide released by the institution over which he presides is getting some bad press—the BFLG, he concedes, is "offensive to many, myself included"—is anyone's guess.

However, given his subsequent comment that "the only NHU policy on speech is that it is free and unfettered on our campus," Huddleston sounds as self-delusional as the authors of the guide who see their work as an intellectual achievement.

"Universities are places to look at the world in new ways," they write in their introduction. "As a university organization, we care about the life of the mind."

As this little guide to "bias-free language" makes clear, this is self-delusion of epic grandeur.

Far from being "places to look at the world in *new ways*," universities generally, and, evidently, the University of New Hampshire specifically, encourage students to look at the world in the same, *old*, unadventurous ways that they have imbibed from the larger culture, a Politically Correct, left-of-center culture for which most contemporary academics insist upon being apologists.

Maybe UNH really does "care" for "the life of the mind."

But it cares to dominate and control the minds of its students.

Jack Kerwick

RELIGION

EVEN AS THE contemporary Western world becomes increasingly secular—even militantly secular, in some locales—religion continues to figure crucially in both the lives of individuals as well as in the life of society. Western civilization continues to draw upon its Christian inheritance in ways often unrecognized by both Christians and non-Christians alike. More specifically, Political Correctness or "progressivism," though generally noted for its hostility toward traditional expressions of Christianity, is actually a variant of it, even if a perverted variant. At the same time, however, far too many clerics and religious leaders make it painfully clear that Political Correctness has informed the Christianity from which it sprung.

That Islam is on the march is still another reason that we can't afford to relegate religion to the periphery. September 11, 2001 made it impossible to ignore the conflict between the Western and Islamic worlds. Far easier to neglect, though, is the unrelenting and unimaginably barbaric oppression that Christians suffer at the hands of Muslims in dozens of Islamic countries around the world.

The articles that follow address some of these issues.

The Christian's Duty to Hate Sin and Evil

There is hardly a week that passes when Christian pastors and ministers from across denominations don't use their time at the pulpit to admonish their flocks to love as Christ loved.

When the Christian world prepares itself for the Passion and Resurrection of its Savior during this Holy Week, such calls to love intensify.

To be certain, Christians are called—are commanded—by their Lord to *love*. As St. Paul said, of the three "theological" virtues, faith, hope, and love, the greatest of these is love.

But those of us who aspire to be the disciples of Jesus are also called to *hate*.

In fact, it is precisely *because* we are called to love that we are called to hate, and to hate with every ounce of the zeal, the devotion, the aching, with which we are expected to love. The paradox here is only apparent:

The love of God and neighbor with which Christians are consumed is inseparable from the intense hatred of evil and sin demanded of them.

Yet Christians hear relatively little about their obligation in Christ to burn with hatred for corruption.

This is nothing short of a scandal.

First, while it is true that, as St. John said in his First Epistle, God *is* Love, it is equally true that God is Justice. The God of the Bible—both the *Old* Testament as well as the *New*—is a God of infinite compassion.

But He is also a God who rewards and punishes.

In stressing God's mercy at the expense of neglecting His wrath, Christians do a gross disservice to both, for divine mercy and divine wrath are meaningful only when each is understood in light of the other.

One can't know God unless one knows about His love *and* His justice.

Second, when justice *is* mentioned in connection with love in many Christian churches nowadays—particularly Roman Catholic churches like the one that I attend—it always refers to something that Christians from times past wouldn't have recognized as justice at all: so-called "*social* justice."

Yet social justice is what I will call *No* Justice. No Justice is a doctrine, favored by secular, atheistic leftists and far too many Christians alike, that the government must confiscate the resources in time, labor, and property from those to whom they belong and "redistribute" them to those who have less. This is the ugly reality of No Justice.

No Justice is injustice. Far from supporting "social justice," as a Christian, I am duty-bound to detest it. And I detest it for the same reason that I detest slavery: it is manifestly unjust for one person or group to coerce others, for whatever reasons, to part with the fruits of their labor.

It is unjust for one person or group to coerce others to subsidize activities to which the latter never consented and to which their consciences may very well be opposed.

But it is exactly this of which No Justice consists.

We should not be misled by any of this into thinking that it is only the evil of the government for which Christians are to reserve their hatred, much less that only government is capable of evil. The disciples of Jesus know as well as anyone that such is the ubiquity of evil in the world that it even infects their own hearts.

Still, while Christian clergy will talk much about sin in the abstract, they seem to studiously avoid mentioning many specifics.

And even when they urge the members of their flocks to look within, they routinely counsel them to be "less judgmental" of others, and more mindful of their own sins. But turning a blind eye to the wickedness of others is a recipe for the perfection, *not* of virtue, but of vice.

It has not infrequently been noted—but not noted enough— that the vicious are a better source of moral guidance than are the virtuous. By way of his life sentence behind bars, a convict stands a far better chance of deterring a reckless adolescent male from a life of crime than that of his honest father who constantly pleads with his beloved son to walk the straight and narrow path.

All of the Surgeon General's warnings regarding the potential dangers of cigarette smoking aren't going to persuade young, healthy smokers from indulging their habit of choice. The sight of a lifelong smoker suffering from lung cancer, however, might do the trick.

Similarly, for Christians to learn about and hate evil as they should, they *must* judge, and judge unequivocally, judge passionately, the wickedness of others. We first spot evil when it is outside of us, and it is vastly easier at that point to recognize it in all of its hideousness.

Noticing and judging the evil of others is an indispensable step to knowing and loving God and neighbor.

Christianity Alive and Well in Our Secular Age

Philadelphia Eagles' star Riley Cooper is the latest celebrity to have to issue an emotional, and very public, mea culpa for having used that most infamous of racial slurs, "the N-word."

Fortunately for him, it appears that Cooper has been forgiven.

From these public apologies much can be learned—and a thing or two about contemporary American racial politics isn't even the most of it.

First, from the highest to the lowest, every aspect of our culture remains saturated in a distinctly *Christian* vision of morality.

The notion that it is gravely immoral to regard people differently, much less treat them badly, on the bases of race, ethnicity, gender, class, and even religion is a part of Christianity's legacy to the world.

And it is the ubiquity of the belief in this idea that accounts for the pressure brought upon Cooper and others to repent of their transgressions.

In other words, if not for the world that Christianity produced, it is not likely that "racism," "sexism," "ethnocentrism," "classism," "ageism," "ableism," "classism," or any of the other "isms" that are deemed unmitigated evils by our public culture would have ever been conceived, to say nothing of actually observed.

Note, I do not mean to suggest that there's anything like a straight line that runs from an educated understanding of Christianity to the Politically Correct excesses of our day. And *I know* that, consciously speaking, the most zealous of "anti-racists" and their ilk are motivated by an *animus* toward Christianity—not a devotion to it.

No matter. The point is that while our PC zeitgeist is doubtless a *perversion* of Christianity, it is still a perversion *of Christianity*. If the aforementioned "isms" are unconscionable, it can only be because the differences on which they are based are *superficial.*

That is, it must be the case that underlying our differences is a common human nature, a fundamental essence from which each and every person derives an inalienable dignity.

It is this belief, and only this belief, that informs not just belief in the awfulness of "racism" and the like.

It is also only this belief that informs the widespread view that there is a "moral law" and "moral rights" of which *all* members of the human race are in possession.

But here's the rub: if there is such a thing as human dignity, then human beings are not, and can never be, the bio-chemical accidents of a purposeless, endless evolutionary process. This isn't to deny evolution, in some sense of this word. It *is* to deny the logical tenability of a theory according to which something called "human dignity" can emerge from a universe comprised of *nothing* but matter in motion.

In fact, as such staunch atheists as Friedrich Nietzsche and Jean Paul Sartre have remarked, the very notion of human nature itself is the offspring of Christianity. The concept of human nature serves the same function as the concept of God: both constrain individuals by specifying in advance limits on what they can do and who they can be. This similarity is no coincidence, for unless there is a God, an author of human nature, the latter can't exist.

But, as Sartre wrote, if there is no God, then "everything is permissible [.]" The great existentialist philosopher admitted that he found this view of reality "very distressing," for he recognized that it entailed that there are "no values or commands" that "legitimize our conduct [.]" It means that "we are alone [.]"

Nietzsche disdainfully referred to Christianity as the penultimate "slave morality" from which other species of slave morality like "Democracy," "socialism," and "liberalism" spun off. From the perspective of "the slave morality," the evil man is "the aristocrat, the powerful one, the one who rules [.]"

The slave-morality, on the other hand, affirms just those qualities that promise to alleviate its proponents' suffering: "sympathy, the kind, helping hand, the warm heart, patience, diligence, humility, and friendliness [.]" Because these are the characteristics that supply "the only means of supporting the burden of existence," they are elevated to the stature of universal human excellences.

If there is such a thing as human dignity, it can only be because humans were, as Christians say, made in the image of God.

The verdict is clear: whether we choose to recognize it or not, the fact of the matter is that upon our shared morality is the indelible impress of Christianity.

The latter's nemeses from yesteryear readily conceded this.

Apparently, their progeny today lack either their ancestors' honesty or their courage.

Christianity and Christmas

Christmas, unlike any other Western holiday, is ubiquitous. It is as impossible for an inhabitant of the Western world to escape Christmas as it is impossible for a person to escape breathing while remaining alive.

For this reason, Christmas is a microscopic expression of Christianity's relationship to the civilization to which it gave rise.

Both religious and irreligious alike celebrate Christmas. Few and far between are the residences, businesses, and even government buildings that aren't adorned with at least some decorative reminders of the season. Christmas music can be heard emanating from every conceivable medium while many television networks and movie theaters are taken over by Christmas-themed programs and films.

While it is true that many of the most widely recognized holiday symbols—talking snowmen, flying reindeer, Christmas trees, candy canes, elves, and even Santa Claus—are "secularized," the religious roots of the holiday are, or at least should be, unmistakable.

For starters, just the word "holiday" itself stems from *holy day,* a day that is supposed to be set aside for prayerful reflection. That, in the Western world, no holiday is as big of a deal as that of Christmas serves as a reminder, however subtle, of the significance of the *holiness* of the occasion.

Secondly, "Christmas" means *the Mass* of *Christ*. With every mention of the word, then, the name of Christ—the "reason for the season"—is invoked.

Thirdly, the very notion, expressed *wherever* there's an expression of Christmas, that Christmas is a cause for celebration, a time for *miracles,* and a time to rejoice in song and gift-giving, derives from no other source other than the traditional Christian belief that God gave us the greatest gift of Himself through the miracle of the Incarnation.

Christmas lights, the stars that we place at the tops of our trees, and even candy canes remind us of this: lights signify *the* Light of Christ; the Christmas tree star beckons back to the star that guided the Magi as they searched for the birth place of baby Jesus; and candy canes are designed to resemble the staff of Jesus, the Good Shepherd, its hardness signifying Jesus, the Rock, and its colors, red and white, pointing, respectively, toward the blood and purity of Christ.

Finally, we mustn't forget that Santa Claus, the most popular and visible of all "secular" symbols of Christmas, is rooted in the historical person of *Saint Nicholas,* a fourth century Christian bishop who, inspired by the example of his Lord and Savior, lived a life of selflessness.

Just as the stuff of which Christmas is made hearken us back to its Christian roots, so too does the stuff of which contemporary *Western civilization* is made hearken us back to *its* Christian roots.

Below are just some of our taken-for-granted ideas and institutions that are unmistakably Christian in origin:

(1) Each and every human being, irrespective of circumstances, possesses an inviolable dignity by virtue of having been created in the image of God. This idea is the core of a moral vision that, unlike its predecessors, extended its liberties and duties to *all* human beings. The tribalism of old had been eclipsed.

(2) Because of (1), we have a duty to extend *charity* to all, including total *strangers,* and even enemies: overwhelmingly, charity is a distinctively *Christian* virtue. This explains why, even at present, charity remains a predominantly Christian phenomenon.

Anthony Esolen, author of The Politically Incorrect Guide to Western Civilization, writes:

> *Hindus do not send holy men into foreign lands to feed the hungry and house the naked: they will not do so for the pariahs in their own land. (emphasis mine).*

He adds:

> *Buddhists, practicing benevolent detachment from the world, do not do so. Muslims, who conquer by force, and who reject natural law on the grounds that it 'fetters' Allah, are required to take care of their own, but they ignore everyone else.*

(3) The world (universe) is not cyclical, as the ancient pagans held, but rational and orderly. It is also not a vale of tears, but, as God declared it, "good." Thus, nature *could be* explored and *should be* explored. From these Christian suppositions, science, with all of its wondrous, life-saving technologies, took flight.

(4) The separation of "Church" and "State" sprung from the Christian's rejection of State worship and, of course, Jesus' admonition to pay unto Caesar his due, while giving God what is owed to *Him*.

(5) Many of the West's most historic philosophers, painters, composers, authors, and scientists derived their inspiration, their presuppositions regarding the characters of ultimate reality, knowledge, religion, and morality from the Christian worldview that they inherited. In the absence of Christianity, it is as inconceivable that our culture would be so much as *remotely* recognizable to itself as it is inconceivable that we would still be celebrating Christmas.

So, this Christmas, let's not only remember that Jesus made possible the occasion for this holiday. Let's remember as well that He made possible the very civilization, the most awesome of civilizations, that we call our own.

Christianity and Inequality

If ever sober-minded folks thought that they could take refuge in the Christian church from the left-wing juggernaut that is our culture's zeitgeist, they can think this no more.

In the vestibule of the Lutheran church in which my son's summer camp is held, I noticed that the most recent edition of *The Lutheran* is devoted to the topic of "economic inequality."

Norma Cook Everist, a professor of church and ministry, quotes Luther who wrote that "the poor" are routinely "defrauded" by the rich. Matters, she declares, are "no less" true "today."

Dividing, as it does, the world into "makers" and "takers," "inequality" fosters the invidious fiction that some, including some people, including "some children," are "worth more than all the rest." This, though, contradicts the Christian's belief that we are all "created in God's image [.]"

"Congregations," Everist writes, "need to welcome, include and minister among people across socioeconomic boundaries." She assures us that "we don't need to fear those named 'of no worth' becoming filled with power and potential because," she concludes, "together we can become life-givers in the world."

Where to begin?

For starters, the term "inequality" when used in this context is both inaccurate and unfair. "Equality" is a morally charged word. In this respect it is not unlike "good," "justice," "virtue," and the like.

Some of "the rich" that Everist and her ilk loathe may know how to cook their books, but Everist and her fellow proponents of economic "equality" most definitely know how to cook their arguments: casting one's position in the language of "equality" is a sure-fire way of stacking the deck in favor of one's view from the outset.

That this is so becomes obvious once it's considered that the very same people who incessantly bemoan "inequality" while arguing for income and wealth redistribution are the first to demand ever greater "diversity." They are the first to bludgeon us into "celebrating" our differences.

Income/wealth "inequality," however, *is* diversity.

If we are going to promote *real* diversity, then it is a foregone conclusion that there will be differences, *dramatic* differences, in the life choices that individuals make.

And this in turn means, necessarily, that there will be staggering differences in the amount of money that people earn, for among the choices that people make throughout their lives is the choice of, well, their livelihoods.

"Inequality," in other words, is just the word that the self-avowed champions of diversity attribute to those instances of diversity that aren't to their liking.

If, as Professor Everist implies, those of us who object to being *coerced* into working longer hours for little to no pay for the sake of realizing the redistributive scheme of some ideologue's imagination are the enemies of "equality," then she and her fellow travelers are the enemies of diversity (to say nothing of individuality and liberty).

Another critical point is that, whether by accident or design, all too many contemporary representatives of the church, like Professor Everist, conflate the issue of "the poor" or "the needy" with that of economic "inequality." In doing so, they radically misconstrue the Gospel.

The parable of the Good Samaritan, *the* parable more than any other designed to emblematize the ideal of Christian charity, features a man of considerable means—the Samaritan—who deployed some of his ample resources to help a stranger in need.

Jesus, in other words, held up a reasonably well-to-do, and possibly even wealthy, man as the model of Christian love.

Christ also praised a Roman soldier, a man, mind you, who was sufficiently well off to have servants, as displaying more faith than *anyone*—including the impoverished to whom He ministered—in all of Israel.

Nicodemus and Joseph of Arimathea were rich members of the priestly class with whom Jesus must've been particularly close, for not only did they attempt to prevail upon their fellow Pharisees to refrain from turning Jesus over to the Romans. Following Jesus' crucifixion, both prepared His body for burial in the tomb that Joseph secured for Him.

The Christian's vocation is to care for *the needy*, for those in need. And this could include *anyone*—regardless of his or her socioeconomic circumstances.

Unfortunately, whether Lutheran, Catholic, or otherwise, the contemporary Christian church's almost exclusive emphasis on "the poor" comes at the cost of reducing the non-poor, and certainly the rich, to the status of non-persons.

As such, the latter are for practical purposes rendered objects, yes, but not proper objects of *agape,* of Christian love.

No, the tireless campaign to demonize "the rich"—as well as those of us who are not rich but who *object* to the demonization of the rich and the socialist fantasies of the demagogues—renders "the rich" just objects.

Of course a great portion of Jesus' ministry was spent ministering to the poor. Yet a great deal was also expended upon attending to the needs of the non-poor—as well as those of *the rich*.

And none of it was spent on the issue of "economic inequality."

Stephen Hawking and Amateur Philosopher Syndrome (APS)

There can be no question that Stephen Hawking is a brilliant scientist.

But he is a lousy philosopher, and an even worse theologian.

If ever it was in question, Hawking's speech at Caltech in April of 2013 established beyond doubt that the world-renowned physicist suffers from Amateur Philosopher Syndrome (APS).

Scientists, particularly popular scientists, like Hawking, are especially prone to APS. All such scientists see the world, not so much scienti*fically,* as scient*istically.* That is, they assume that there is but one legitimate tongue in which to speak of reality: the language of science. All others are dismissed.

Three aspects of Hawking's lecture reveal his to be a classic textbook case of APS.

First, while referring to this as a "glorious time" in which we have succeeded in coming "this close to an understanding of the laws governing us and our universe," Hawking referred to human beings as but "*mere* collections of fundamental particles of nature" (emphasis added)[.]

Second, as The Daily Mail reported on Thursday, Hawking mocked "the religious position" on the origins of the universe by likening it to "the myth of an African tribe whose God vomited the Sun, Moon, and stars."

Finally, Hawking assured his audience that, thanks to "general relativity" and "quantum theory," we can now account for the origins of the universe without any appeals to God at all: our universe, like one foamy bubble among countless others, might just be one of an infinite number of other universes.

To the first point, the question must be posed: From whence springs the assumption that we are "*mere*" combinations of physical particles? There are at least two problems with a scientist using the word "mere."

The first is that "mere" is an evaluative, not a descriptive, a philosophical, not a scientific, term.

As Hawking uses it, is likely intended as a *meta*physical—not a *physical*—word. It suggests *insignificance*. But, scientifically speaking, it is as inappropriate to speak of the significance or insignificance of the world as it is to speak of its beauty and ugliness, or its sweetness and bitterness.

These are not attributes of the universe; they are attributes of *our minds* that we *project* onto the world.

The second problem is that "mere" is exhaustive.

To say that X is "merely" this or that is to say that it is *only* this or that. Science—real science, not philosophical or ideological dogma masquerading as science—can't speak to ultimate questions.

That's the job of philosophy and theology. Science can determine that we are bundles of material particles, but it most definitely cannot determine whether we are merely this.

What stuns most of all is just how illiterate in the philosophical and theological traditions of Western civilization Hawking appears.

For millennia, Jews and (later) Christians have found the idea of God "vomiting" the universe to be just as primitive, just as crass, as it strikes Hawking as being. The reason for this is not hard to grasp: if God puked up the universe, then He didn't *create* it.

Jews are unique in world history in being the first to affirm the existence of one supreme God who *created* the world *out of nothing*.

This is crucial, for it is this belief that the world is distinct from, yet created in the image of, an all-good and all-wise being, from which the scientific enterprise was born. As long as the world is thought of as a distinct creation of God, it is assumed to be both rational and good, i.e. a proper object of study.

In short, neither science nor the scientist Stephen Hawking

ever would have arisen had it not been for this conception of divine creation that Hawking ridicules without having grasped.

There is one last point that bears mentioning.

The notion of a sea of "universes" that Hawking invokes is both logically troublesome and theologically irrelevant. The word "universe" is a synonym for "everything."

So, claiming that there is an infinite number of "universes" makes about as much sense as claiming that there is an infinite number of "everythings."

But even if there is some sense to be had from the idea of multiple universes, and even if these universes have always existed, this doesn't for a moment circumvent the fundamental question: why is there something rather than nothing? *This* is what we want to know when we ask about the beginning of the universe.

And, contrary to Hawking, explaining the existence of a universe by referring back, and only back, to the universe itself is like accounting for one's own existence by looking no further than oneself.

The verdict: Hawking hasn't come close to showing that we can dispense with the God hypothesis in explaining the presence of the universe.

The Legacy of Christianity

A group that refers to itself as the "Arkansas Society of Freethinkers" is not in the Christmas spirit. When it caught wind of the fact that Little Rock's Terry Elementary School arranged for its students to attend a stage performance of "A Charlie Brown Christmas" at a local church, it began to eye the school up for a lawsuit.

Inasmuch as one of its key characters quotes the Gospel of Luke, "A Charlie Brown Christmas," you see, has an explicitly religious theme.

That there is no such "separation" clause in the United States Constitution has long been established. Yet this episode is telling not because it reveals the atheist's ignorance of the Constitution. Rather, it is telling insofar as it reveals his ignorance of his cultural inheritance.

The great Catholic writer, Hilaire Belloc, had famously declared that "the faith is Europe and Europe is the faith." We can paraphrase him by saying just as assuredly that Christianity is the West and the West is Christianity.

It is true that the Western mind is indebted to classical, pre-Christian Greek and Roman sources, but even here, it is primarily to Christian men of learning to whom we owe thanks for resurrecting and restoring to European civilization the lost riches of antiquity.

For the last two millennia there has been no aspect of Western existence that hasn't borne upon it the indelible impress of the Christian religion.

Take science. That it is the Western world within which the sciences first emerged and where they continue to flourish is no coincidence. Prior to the rise of Judaism (from which Christianity spun off), and outside of the Christian West to this day, time is conceived cyclically, not linearly. But it is our linear conception of time that inspires the scientist's faith in the possibility of achieving progress within his craft.

There are still other distinctively Christian concepts from which science has taken flight.

That the universe has been created by an all-good God and that this God has entrusted its care to the custody of human beings render it impossible for those who've been influenced by these beliefs to deny the reality of the world, as do Hindus and Buddhists, or to assume an attitude of indifference toward it, as did the Stoics.

These Christian beliefs make it impossible to proclaim, with Plato and his disciples, that matter is somehow debased and, thus, unworthy of investigation. They make it impossible to deny the rationality of the world and, hence, the knowledge to be gotten from it.

The very (scientific) enterprise at which the scientist makes his living would have been unthinkable in the absence of the religious faith that he now ignores, and—far too frequently—disdains.

Furthermore, he continues to erect his monuments upon the back of the Christian faith, for the supposition that nature is knowable and worth studying makes sense only within the context of Christianity. But once it has been plucked from that framework, then it is about as meaningful as a piece of a puzzle without the puzzle to which it belongs.

And what is true of the ideas underlying science are no less true of those of our morality.

The famed Russian novelist Dostoyevsky had said that if there is no God, then all things are possible. Dostoyevsky was a Christian. Yet some honest atheists—like the existentialist philosopher, Jean Paul Sartre—have admitted that he was correct.

"Indeed," Sartre wrote, it is precisely because "everything is permissible if God does not exist" that existentialist atheists like himself find life "very distressing [.]" Since there is no God, "all possibility of finding values in a heaven of ideas disappears along with Him [.]" There are "no values or commands" that "legitimize our conduct," there is "no excuse behind us, nor justification before us," for "we are alone...."

If Christianity is to go the way of the dinosaur, so too must natural law, natural rights, human rights, the Good, the True, and the Beautiful, and each and every one of our traditional moral ideals go this route, for without the theological *gestalt* supplied by Christianity, these ideals are reduced to arbitrary human inventions.

This Christmas season, let the "free thinkers" among us recognize that nothing that we take for granted—including our thought—is free. The price we pay for the goods we value is civilization, and for this civilization of ours we owe an eternal debt of gratitude to the very religion that too many of our "free thinkers" are intent upon destroying.

Obama's Historical Illiteracy Regarding the Crusades

It's a sad commentary on our time that *anyone*, to say nothing of the President of the United States of America, would so much as *think*, much less publicly announce, that there is some sort of moral equivalence between the contemporary phenomenon of Islamic barbarity and such oft-cited examples of Western and American injustices as the Crusades, slavery, and Jim Crow. Some comments are in order.

First, critics who make the "That Was Then, This Is Now," argument against Obama not only sorely miss the point; they actually *legitimize* his contention that Christians *are* guilty of the charge that Obama levels against them.

The truth is that while *individual* Crusaders, like individual soldiers in every war, were indeed guilty of some horrible things, the Crusades *as such* were just. Obama typifies the Christophobe who can't resist treating the Crusades as an axiomatic instance of Christian villainy while conveniently refusing to mention that they were a response to *centuries* of *Islamic* aggression.

That's right: For *centuries* Islamic armies had been *conquering* Christian lands generally and the Holy Land specifically. And the invasion into Europe was well underway by the time Urban II issued a call for the first holy war in 1095.

"From the confines of Jerusalem and from the city of Constantinople," the Pope exclaimed, "a grievous report has gone forth [.]" The word was indeed "grievous," for "a race from the kingdom of Persians," what the Pope characterized as "an accursed race," "has violently invaded the lands" of Christians "and has depopulated them by pillage and fire."

These Persians—Muslims—"have led away a part of the captives into their own country, and a part," he says, "they have killed by cruel tortures." Churches had been destroyed and "the kingdom of the Greeks" has been "dismembered" and "deprived of territory so vast in extent that it could not be traversed in two months' time."

Obama is right that the Crusades most certainly were conducted by Christians in the name of Christ. But unless defending one's person and property against those who mean to deprive one of them is immoral, the Crusades *per se* amounted to an eminently just enterprise. That abuses and even atrocities occurred in the Crusades no more establishes the injustice of the Crusades *as such* than does the fact that abuses, and even atrocities, occur within marriages and families establish the immorality of marriage and family *as such.*

Second, slavery had been a global institution from time out of mind. In the Christian world, and in America, slavery was not conducted "in the name of Christ," as Obama maintains.

It's true that slave owners, including and especially *Christian* slave owners, frequently alluded to the Bible to show that the *fanatical* abolitionists' charge that slavery was a *sin* was unsustainable. However, many of these same Christian slave holders nevertheless believed that slavery *was* an evil that needed to be abolished.

Even still, only a woefully impoverished moral imagination could fail to recognize the relevant differences between, on the one hand, the situation of slavery in which earlier generations of Americans found themselves, to say nothing of the situation of Jim Crow (!) that Americans eradicated more recently, and, on the other, the situation that ISIS and other Islamic jihadists are creating for their victims whenever and wherever they rear their beastly heads.

Indeed, such is the sophomoric character of Obama's moral

vision that it would be laughable if it weren't so damned offensive—and dangerous: in one and the same breath, he speaks of *both* a white segregationist's refusal to associate with blacks *and* an Islamic fanatic's refusal to grant mercy to a person who he instead cages and eventually *burns to death*.

Third, more galling than Obama's historical illiteracy and moral idiocy is his rank hypocrisy.

Though he talks of "we" when implying moral parity between Islamic violence and the violence perpetrated by Christians in the past, Obama most certainly does *not* mean what he says. What he is *really* saying is that *you*—*all* of you *white Christians*—must not shed any of that *white guilt* that's paid off so well for the Barack Obamas of the world.

Let's be frank: Leftists like Obama have been able to perpetuate the fiction—the invidious fiction—that, to paraphrase one of his fellow leftists, the white race is "the cancer" of the planet, by ignoring the evils committed by the world's peoples of color.

For you see, when the historical conduct of whites is compared with, not contemporary Western standards, but the historical—and *present*—conduct of *all* peoples, it becomes crystal clear that the injustices for which whites, and white Christians in particular, are forever being blamed and for which they are forever atoning are common to the human species.

But more than this, remarkably, it is only among whites, and especially among white Christians, that a genuine moral revulsion of these perennial practices arose. Whites, especially white Christians, though the majority and the wielders of power in the West, made enormous sacrifices to rectify not just those wrongs that were done to *fellow white Christians;* but as well those wrongs suffered by *non-whites and non-Christians*, both in the West and *beyond*.

Obama and his ilk in the Racism-Industrial-Complex have too much to lose if this dirty little secret gets out.

It is this, more so than anything else, that explains why, in the light of the Islamic savagery on display in the fatal burning of a Jordanian pilot, Obama *had* to warn us against getting on "*our* high horse."

The Truth about Christ

The Christian world just celebrated the Easter holiday, the Resurrection of Jesus, the God-Man, from the dead. Yet there are many people who either don't believe in God or, if they do, certainly don't believe that the Supreme Being assumed flesh in the person of Jesus of Nazareth.

At the same time, however, they hold the man Jesus in high regard, either reinterpreting many of His remarks or explaining them away as inventions of later generations.

Neither approach succeeds.

Antony Flew is a world leading philosopher who died at the ripe old age of 87 just a few years ago.

For over 50 years, Flew was recognized for being among the profession's most powerful *critics* of theism (belief in God). Such was the relentlessness and force of Flew's arguments that he is credited by his colleagues—both theist and atheist alike—with having virtually revolutionized the field of the philosophy of religion.

Within the last decade or so, Flew—a paragon of intellectual honesty—concluded that all of this time, *he had been wrong*.

Though he never became a Christian—the belief *that* God exists is *not* equivalent to belief *in* God, much less belief in *Christ*—he came to think that among the world's religious traditions, none is as intriguing, as alluring, as Christianity.

"Today," Flew states, "I would say that the claim concerning the resurrection is more impressive than any by the religious competition," and that made on behalf of the Incarnation "unique." He admits to believing that more so than any other religion, Christianity "deserves to be honored and respected"—regardless of whether it is the "divine revelation" that it claims to be. "There is nothing like" its "combination of a charismatic figure like Jesus and a first-class intellectual like St. Paul."

The latter, Flew asserts, "had a brilliant philosophical mind and could both speak and write in all the relevant languages."

In his book, *There is A God,* Flew shares his correspondence with one the world's most seasoned and respected of New Testament scholars, N.T. Wright.

Flew admits to being "very much impressed" with Wright's argument(s) for the Incarnation and Resurrection of Christ, calling his approach "enormously important," "absolutely wonderful, absolutely radical, and very powerful."

Wright grounds his "faith in Jesus as the incarnate Son of God," not in the Gospels, but in the way and ways in which "first-century Jews understood God and God's action in the world." This Jewish understanding, in turn, was anchored in the Hebrew Scriptures, i.e. The Old Testament. Jews, Wright reminds us, "talk[ed] about the Word of God," "the wisdom of God," "the glory of God dwelling in the Temple," "the law of God," and "the spirit of God."

Wright notes that when we turn to the Gospels, what we find is "Jesus behaving—not just talking, but behaving—as if somehow those five ways [of talking about God] are coming true in a new manner in what he is doing." In other words, Jesus behaves and talks as if He believed that "he was called to *embody* the return of Yahweh to Zion" (italics original).

Since "embody" is the English equivalent of the Latin "incarnation," the point is that, on Wright's reading, Jesus indeed conceived Himself as the incarnation of Israel's *God.*

Lest the skeptic think that Wright—a universally esteemed biblical scholar, mind you—is just another incorrigibly prejudiced Christian, he calls upon Jacob Neusner, a prominent *Jewish* scholar who concurs with Wright's interpretation.

In addition to his numerous books on Judaism, Neusner also authored a book on Christianity. "In it," Wright says, Neusner remarked "that when he reads that Jesus said things like, 'You have heard that it was said thus and so, but I say unto you this and this and this,' 'I want to say to this Jesus: Who do you think you are? God?'"

C. S. Lewis wasn't the first to articulate what has since come to be known as "Lewis' *Trilemma*." As the 19th century Scottish preacher John Duncan said: "Christ either deceived mankind by conscious fraud, or He was Himself deluded and self-deceived, or He was Divine. There is no getting out of this trilemma. It is inexorable."

Jesus: No Radical

Recently, while discussing topics in the philosophy of religion during my introductory course in philosophy, a student claimed that Jesus was "a rebel." Although this judgment of hers is not without some truth, it is decidedly false in the sense in which I am sure she intended for it to be taken.

The idea that Jesus was a rebel or radical is certainly an improvement over the "meek and mild" Jesus of the popular imagination. The latter is a neutered Jesus, a Jesus that functions as a blank screen upon which anyone and everyone can project his theological, moral, and political idiosyncrasies. The former, in contrast, is a being with passion and conviction.

Still, in the sense in which it is commonly used, the sense in which my student used it, the image of Jesus as rebel is as much of a fiction as is that of Jesus meek and mild.

Many contemporary New Testament scholars have labored hard to promote this depiction of Jesus as a radical or rebel. While I lack their professional expertise, as a Christian, I can confidently reject their reading of the Scriptures.

The problem with the words "rebel" and "radical" lies in their connotations. More often than not, they are explicitly *political*. And even when they aren't *explicitly* political, they are *implicitly* as much, for they suggest a figure whose critical eye is forever set upon a culture.

Those scholars and laypersons who are fond of referring to Jesus as "a rebel" or "radical" know this. *This is why they do it.*

By casting Jesus as a "radical," those students of the Bible whose sympathies lie with the politics of the left—i.e. *most* of those who characterize Jesus as a "radical"—hope to link Him with their own ideological causes and commitments.

For example, Jesus, they say, was a champion of "social justice." Those who do not consciously subscribe to leftist politics, on the other hand, have their own reasons for seeing Jesus as a "radical": they want their Christianity—and, thus, their Christ— to have political relevance.

In any case, *if* we insist on viewing Jesus as a rebel, then we must be clear as to what He was and was not rebelling against.

Jesus was not an "anti-imperialist" rebelling against imperial Rome. Nor was He an "egalitarian" interested in "deconstructing" those "social structures" designed to perpetuate "asymmetries" of "*power*" between "the haves" and "the have nots." Jesus was not in the least concerned with dismantling "patriarchy" or "classism."

If Jesus was a rebel, it was against *sin* or *evil* that he railed.

To put this point another way, any portrait of Jesus that isn't *theological* is *not* a portrait of Jesus.

Only in light of Jesus' *cosmic* vocation do both the Gospels as well as the rise of Christianity become intelligible.

Jesus did indeed want to change the world—but one heart at a time. For utopian political schemes of the sort that were all too common during His day—and ours—Jesus had no use. Not only did He repudiate those who envisioned the Messiah as a figure who would wrest all power away from Rome and restore Israel to some idyllic condition. Jesus said remarkably little about Rome at all, and what He did say wasn't remotely subversive, or even angry.

Recall that when Jesus healed the centurion's servant, He did not first demand of Him that the soldier relinquish his duties. He praised the centurion for his faith. He criticized neither the centurion nor the Roman Empire of which he was an agent.

In fact, unlike—radically unlike—those contemporary leftist activists who style themselves inheritors of a prophetic tradition of advocating on behalf of the oppressed and subjugated, Jesus was not infrequently as harsh with His most devoted disciples as He was His enemies within the Jewish ruling class. But I suppose that this is the point: Jesus had *disciples;* today's activists have *constituents.*

Jesus never would have permitted—never did permit—His disciples to invoke their poverty or their condition of living under Roman occupation (or the occupation of *any* foreign power) as justification for impiety—much less the sorts of egregious conduct that many of today's "poor" engage in and for which they are excused by their self-appointed champions.

No, Jesus was no radical or rebel. He was not a visionary or champion of "social justice." He wasn't interested in dissolving all class distinctions and ushering in a property-less Eden on Earth.

Jesus was the Son of God. He was interested first and foremost in prevailing over sin and evil, through violence, yes, but the violence that He would permit to be inflicted upon Himself.

Jesus was the Christ, the Son of the Living God, as Peter said. He became one of us so that He could redeem humanity and transform us into the adopted sons and daughters of God the Father.

No other understanding of Jesus is adequate.

Pope Francis: Communist?

Pope Francis is once again insisting that he is not a communist, that his abiding concern for "the poor" is grounded in the Gospel of Christ, not the ideology of Marx, Engels, or any other communist.

Back in 2010, while still a Cardinal, he felt the need to do the same.

Why?

It may very well be inaccurate to describe the Pope as a communist. But—and it pains this Catholic writer to admit this—one can be forgiven for suspecting that he is friendlier to this noxious ideology than many of us would care to think.

First, neither Francis' recent remarks nor those from 2010 include an express repudiation of communism. That his concern for the poor reflects Francis' commitment to Christianity in no way speaks to his thoughts on communism. Logically, subscription to one theory is perfectly compatible with respect for and appreciation of any number of others—and it certainly doesn't entail an unqualified rejection of all others.

That is, one can believe that Christianity contains "the fullness of truth" while simultaneously affirming what truth is found in other systems of thought. St. Augustine and St. Thomas Aquinas are two notable examples of Christian thinkers who did precisely this vis-à-vis the philosophies of Plato and Aristotle, respectively.

Similarly, while Francis derives his motivation from Christianity, this doesn't necessarily mean that he cannot and/or does not sympathize with communism.

Secondly, "communism" can mean different things to different people. For instance, Martin Luther King, Jr. denied that he was a communist on the grounds that he rejected "*materialism*," the philosophical doctrine that *matter* is all that there is, the doctrine underwriting Marxism.

However, to reject Marx's theory of *communism*, much less his theory of materialism, does not translate into a rejection of communism as such. To suggest otherwise is like saying that if I reject Calvin's theology of Christianity, I must reject Christianity as such.

The closest Francis has come to criticizing communism is when he articulated a heavily qualified criticism of "liberation theology," a hard leftist approach to Christianity. And even then, the Pope simply noted that its "Marxist interpretation of reality"—again, whatever exactly this means—was a "limitation" while *commending* liberation theology for "its positive aspects."

When communism is understood as most of us understand it, as an ideology demanding a radical redistribution of goods for the purposes of "Equality" or "Fairness" or whatever, then it should be obvious that it can afford to dispense with philosophical materialism and even its "Marxist interpretation of reality."

In other words, "Christian communism" is not a *meaningless* moniker.

That the Pope has refused to unabashedly, unequivocally repudiate communism (and/or socialism) is doubtless one big reason that some have viewed him as a communist sympathizer. Yet there is another: his Holiness *has* adamantly repudiated that system commonly called "capitalism."

Now, Francis' supporters have leapt to his defense on this score. For example, the Catholic writer Selwyn Duke has observed that Francis has never critiqued "capitalism" by name, but instead has simply called for "a God-centered ethics." Daniel Doherty writes that while the Pope is critical of "unfettered capitalism and capitalism generally," his remarks on these matters "hardly" constitute "a clarion call for Marxist revolution [.]"

What Duke and Doherty say of the Pope can be said just as easily of any Democratic politician in the United States. Democrats, especially among election time when they are busy courting the Christian vote, spare no occasion to put a Gospel dress on their socialism—all the while refraining from criticizing "capitalism" by name. They are all in favor of "a God-centered ethic" then.

There is more. This Pope has made comments regarding our economic system that can and have been made quite frequently by socialists of various stripes.

For one, he has blasted "trickle-down economics" for its "crude and naïve trust in the goodness of those wielding economic power and in the sacralized workings of the prevailing economic system."

Of course, in the real world, "trickle-down economics" hasn't a single defender. The only people who speak as if the term had a referent are the socialist-minded.

Francis has also referred to ours as "an economy of exclusion and inequality." "Today," he explains, "everything comes under the laws of competition and the survival of the fittest, where the powerful feed upon the powerless. As a consequence," Francis concludes, "masses of people find themselves excluded and marginalized: without work, without possibilities, without any means of escape."

Where have we heard this lingo before?

In fact, Francis has spoken out more forcefully than Obama or any other Democrat against our economy when he charged it with violating the commandment against *killing*. "Such an economy," Francis insists, "*kills*" (emphasis added).

Though painful for people to admit it, the truth is that Pope Francis is no friend to the liberty that some of us Americans still treasure.

Jesus and Pope Francis

In his speech for the Catholic Church's World Day of Peace, marked for New Year's Day, *Time's* most recently elected "Person of the Year" decried the "widening gap between those who have more and those who must be content with the crumbs."

Pope Francis, it is obvious, is hammering the same theme that he sounded a few weeks ago when he called upon the world to reject "trickle-down economics," "an economy of exclusion and inequality," for "such an economy," he informed us, "kills."

The left is thrilled by this Pope's remarks. As a traditional, practicing Roman Catholic Christian and lover of liberty, I decidedly am not.

While Pope Francis is correct to admonish us to condemn murderous economies, what he is describing doesn't exist. Furthermore, we must grasp that he articulates not the cardinal tenet of Christian charity, but an ideology of welfare-state socialism.

Contrary to what many a contemporary cleric would have us think, Jesus never once—never ever—spoke about the need for His disciples to "narrow the gap" in "income" and "wealth" between "the rich" and "the poor." He never once deplored "inequality," for He came not in the service of an ideology of Equality, but in the service of saving humanity from its sins. The only "economy" in which Jesus ever expressed an interest is the economy of *salvation*.

Of course, this does *not* mean that Christians should be indifferent to the world's affairs generally, and "economies" that "kill" in particular. What it most certainly *does* mean is that if it is the latter that our discipleship calls upon us to resist, then it is on just *those* economies, those "systems," that we must set our sights.

And "the free market" ain't one of them.

At a minimum, within "capitalist" orders, standards of living for *all* have risen to an extent that even the nobility of earlier times never could have imagined. The poor has nowhere been better served than in such societies. At the same time, it is economies of the kind on behalf of which the Pope advocates— particularly those within which there exists an obsession with promoting greater material "equality"—that have eventuated in greater rates of suffering and death.

"Capitalism" is indeed deserving of its share of criticism. But socialism is deserving of a significantly larger share.

Christian charity is doubtless among the noblest, most beautiful things to have ever graced this fallen world of ours. As much as its critics hate to admit it, the fact is that the vast majority of the planet's charitable organizations, and all of the most influential of such organizations, are inspired by the person of Christ: charity—love—is the greatest of commandments for the disciples of Jesus.

However, Jesus was clear that charity is not defined by *material conditions*. Those "in need" can and not infrequently *are* from *all walks of life*. If being alive for more than a handful of years isn't enough to convince people of this, then maybe some reminders of the fact that Jesus befriended, and served, the wealthy, as well as the poor, the powerful, as well as the powerless, might do the trick.

Christ, let us not forget, not only healed the servant of a Roman centurion; He commended the soldier—an agent of *the Roman Empire,* mind you—for having more faith than that of *anyone* that He had encountered up to that point in Israel.

It is crucial to grasp that this incident with the (relatively wealthy) Roman soldier was no fluke: in spite of the sense of His fellow Jews that they were living under oppressive foreign rule, and in spite of the fact that Christ Himself was eventually executed by Rome, He never once so much as critiqued the Roman government—while He tirelessly critiqued the children of Israel.

Jesus never condemned human slavery, and even told parables featuring slaves and slave masters, parables suggesting that slave masters had authority (even if qualified by God's authority) over their slaves.

He as well told a parable of an employer in which he clearly affirmed the employer's right to pay his laborers just the wage that they agreed to be paid—regardless of whether he chose to pay other laborers differently, or *unequally*.

The point here isn't that Jesus was an advocate for slavery, "capitalism," or any other "ism." The point is that He was *not* an advocate of any.

Jesus was concerned not with changing "super structures," "systems," "states," and/or "economies." He was concerned with changing people's hearts. Perhaps He realized that focus on the former detracts from focus on the latter.

Pope Francis and people everywhere would be well served to realize this as well.

Who Really Faces an Existential Threat? Christians Living in Islamic Lands

In spite of what Barack Obama would have us believe, he was as much in tune to Benjamin Netanyahu's address to Congress this week as was anyone and everyone else in the world.

But *exclusive* focus on American/Israeli and Israeli/Islamic relations threatens to blind us to the fierce, unrelenting oppression with which Christians throughout the world are routinely forced to reckon courtesy of their Islamic neighbors.

Throughout the Islamosphere in Africa and the Middle East, men, women, and *children* have been subjected en masse to unspeakable acts of cruelty.

Jihadists, while pillaging and burning homes and churches, have laid waste to whole communities.

Families have been destroyed as husbands and fathers were bludgeoned, beheaded, and burned to death; wives and mothers raped, beaten, and starved; young boys forced to convert to Islam and take up arms on behalf of their captors; and young girls enslaved and sold off to become either wives to grown men or human missiles—i.e. suicide bombers.

Meanwhile, stateside, the historical and theological illiterates of the left—exemplified by none other than our 44th President—spout as a matter of course vacuities designed to imply moral parity between Islam and other religions. Worse, the American left reserves not a fraction of the condemnation for Islam, or even ISIS, that it regularly unleashes on Christianity.

But there is *no* moral parity here.

And it is profoundly offensive for anyone, least of all self-avowed Christian leaders, to suggest otherwise.

People like none other than the titular head of my church, Pope Francis, sought an explanation for the mass murderers that attacked Charlie Hebdo that came dangerously close to sounding like a justification.

To be clear, the Pope doubtless abhorred this ghastly deed as much as anyone. But he expressed an understanding of these Islamic killers that he never would have dreamt of extending to Christians whose sins were far less grave.

That there is a glaring contrast between Christianity and Islam is gotten quickly enough when we consider just how the legions of Christian victims of Islamic persecution have responded to their tormentors.

In Niger, where ISIS incinerated 45 churches, the Christians who survived the rampages (which left at least 10 dead and roughly another 170 people critically injured) still managed to gather to worship together. According to The Voice of the Martyrs, a teenager remarked: "I guess God found us worthy."

Open Doors reports that following the beheadings of 21 Coptic Christian by ISIS, churches in Egypt "united" to pray *for the murderers.*

This organization dedicated to serving persecuted Christians shares a letter penned by an Egyptian "Christian leader" whose name remains anonymous. "The sound of prayers requesting mercy and life, not revenge and destruction, calling on God's name to come and change the hearts of the killers, is loudly heard across Egypt."

The letter relays that the "heartbroken wives, mothers, fathers and children of the martyrs," while interviewed on national and other television shows, offered "simple expressions of love and forgiveness" that "brought down so many tears on air and surely delivered a mind blowing message about what the Christian faith is all about."

Pastors of Egyptian churches are "calling their congregations to wake up and pray for the persecutors of the church to come to meet with the Savior" so that "God will remove their stone hearts…and give them hearts of flesh and blood, capable of loving."

Organizations like Open Doors and Voice of the Martyrs ask Christians around the world not to take up arms and avenge their subjugated brethren, but, rather, to pray for them.

The Christian News Wire reports that Christian Freedom International asked three Christians from three different Muslim-majority countries about their thoughts on Obama's National Prayer Breakfast remarks. Their responses are telling.

A Pakistani Christian replied: "I strongly condemn this statement by US President Obama…Christianity has always preached to love our neighbor." The person added: "I know of no Christian extremist groups attacking people of other faiths."

An Egyptian Christian said that he or she—the lives of these believers depend upon their anonymity—disagreed with Obama. "Coptic Christians in Egypt are very much pacifists and considered the most vulnerable minority [.]"

Thus, "we cannot persecute people of other faiths. We Christians do not persecute Muslims. But we Christians are persecuted."

A *Muslim convert* to Christianity living in Bangladesh had some particularly revealing things to say.

"But, the basic difference [between Christians and Muslims] is that Muslims today are being influenced and taught by their religious books to persecute the people of other beliefs."

In contrast, you can't find "a single word in the New Testament that influences Christians to persecute others. The New Testament teaches [about] loving others."

This convert from Islam mentions that while Christianity has produced numerous people, like Mother Teresa, who have made enormous sacrifices to serve others, "there is not a single example in the Muslim World of a Mother Teresa." Instead, "Muslims have examples like Osama bin Laden."

This person doesn't stop here though. He or she identifies as the inspiration for Obama's comments an Indian Muslim scholar by the name of Dr. Zakir Nayak. The latter, according to this irate Christian, "defends al Qaida activities by saying, 'Christians and Jews did terrible things in the past.'" Obama, he thinks, was exposed to Nayak while in India.

At any rate, this interviewee poses a "challenge" to Obama to "find a single word in the New Testament that influences people to persecute others, where there are thousands [of such words] in the Muslim book, Quran."

If Islamic militants can be said to pose an "existential threat" to anyone today, it is to those Christians living in Islamic lands.

Only don't expect for Obama or John Kerry to ever bring this up.

Why Do They Hate Us? Because We are not Them

Since at least the time of the outset of the Iraq War—and quite possibly well before then—there has been much debate among those to the right over *why* Islamic militants have set their sights upon America and the West.

George W. Bush expressed the consensus among most Republican politicians and commentators when he remarked that they hate us because of our *values.*

Ron Paul, in contrast, represents most libertarians when he

attributes to America's enemies a hatred of, not American liberties, but American *foreign policy*.

Both groups are both right and wrong. For failing to see this, they argue past one another.

Paul, Pat Buchanan, and others are indeed correct when they note that jihadists in places like Iraq and other Middle Eastern lands despise America because of what has been called an "interventionist" foreign policy.

Yet they are mistaken—sorely mistaken—insofar as they assume that *if only* America *disappeared* from the Islamic world, so too would our problems with Islamic violence *disappear*.

Republicans too are correct in charging jihadists with despising American and Western *values*.

But they are incorrect inasmuch as they imply that Islamic militants have a problem with liberty, equality, etc. *as such*.

In other words, they are incorrect insofar as they imply that it is the specific *content* of these value that elicit the homicidal ire of jihadists.

The latter certainly do hate our values. But that's only because they are *our* values—and not *theirs*.

In short, they hate our values because they are not *Islamic* values.

And this gets to the heart of the matter: the "Bush" and "Paul" camps argue past one another because both fail to reckon with the role played by *Islam*—not "Islamism," "Islamo-Fascism," "Islamo-Nazism," "radical Islam," "Islamic extremism," or some other politically acceptable fiction, but Islam—in these violent clashes with Muslims.

Muslims around the world routinely engage in unspeakable acts of cruelty toward their neighbors in contexts that obviously have *nothing whatsoever to do* with American values, American foreign policy, or, for that matter, *America*.

The fierce persecution of Christians courtesy of their Muslim neighbors is an epidemic—and yet it is among the least talked about forms of contemporary oppression.

In Nigeria, for instance, the persecution is "extreme," according to Open Doors, an organization dedicated to combating anti-Christian persecution. There are 183 million Nigerians, of which 89 million are Christian. Yet Boko Haram—an Islamic militant outfit—has rendered peaceful co-existence impossible.

In northeastern Nigeria, Muslims have declared a caliphate. Hundreds of children, boys and girls, as well as women have been abducted, and thousands more have been rendered homeless upon the destruction of their homes. In the twelve northern *Sharia* states, Christians have been all but squeezed out.

Oliver Dashe Doeme of Maiduguri, a bishop and the head of a diocese in northeastern Nigeria, gave an interview with *Catholic On-Line*. He relays how over the last five years, Muslims have all but reduced his diocese to ashes. Over 50 churches and chapel have been ruined, and hundreds have been abandoned. Worse of all, more than *1,000* Catholics have been *murdered.*

The Bishop reports that Catholics are forced at gun-point or knife-point to convert to Islam. If they fail to do so, they are slaughtered.

For the sake of saving the lives of Christians, not just in Nigeria, but in the region, he pleads with "Western powers" to intervene. Only something of a military onslaught against Boko Haram can stop it, he believes.

But it isn't just the Christians of Nigeria that agonize at the hands of Muslims. Nigerians have it bad: according to Open Doors, out of 50 countries worldwide, Nigeria is the tenth worse place for Christians. And it's true that Muslims aren't the *only* persecutors of Christians.

But in 40 of the Earth's 50 countries where Christians are made to suffer because of their faith, Muslims are the culprits.

Open Doors evaluates global persecution of Christians in terms of degrees. The worst is "extreme persecution." Eleven countries are named here. In 10 of these, the persecutors are

Islamic. The second worst type of Christian persecution is "severe persecution." In 11 of 14 countries, the culprits are Islamic. Next there is "moderate persecution." In 10 of 14 countries, those responsible for the persecution are largely Islamic.

Finally, there is "sparse persecution."

In nine of 11 countries, Muslims engage in the persecution of Christians.

In none of these instances of Islamic violence and oppression does "American values" or American foreign policy play a role.

Islam, however, most certainly does.

RACE

IN AMERICA TODAY, it is scarcely possible to get through a single day without hearing about "racism." To listen to the conventional wisdom, one must conclude that "racism" is at once ubiquitous and particularly, maybe even uniquely, awful. And the charge of "racism" is the nuclear bomb of all allegations: the mere charge is enough to shatter lives and ruin reputations. Actually, the indictment of "racism" is all but guaranteed to destroy the lives of whites, for in our topsy-turvy political universe, "racism" is treated synonymously with "white racism." Blacks and other non-whites are all but immunized against the charge.

This is especially troubling in the case of blacks: of the 1.7 million interracial crimes that occur each year, 1.2 million involve black perpetrators. In other words, nearly 90% of interracial crime involves black criminals and non-white, but mostly white, victims.

The fiction that blacks specifically, and non-whites generally, are made to endure unrelenting white oppression serves the interests of what I refer to as the "Racism-Industrial-Complex" (RIC). Materially, ideologically, and politically, this fiction has had an incalculable pay off for those who peddle it. In the name of combatting "racism," the federal government has become a colossus: there is no limit to the power that it will assume for the sake of insuring "racial equality." In the meantime, more individual liberties are lost and the everyday realities, like the everyday reality of black underclass pathology, with which

Americans have to contend are ignored by the movers and shakers of public opinion who stand to gain from the RIC narrative of perpetual White Oppression and Black Suffering.

The articles that follow expose these gross double standards for what they are.

Standing with Charlie Hebdo? A Study in American Hypocrisy

You hypocrite, first take the log out of your own eye, and then you will see clearly to take the speck out of your neighbor's eye. (Mt. 7:5).

Listening to the American media coverage—particularly the coverage of those in the "alternative media"—of the latest outburst of Islamic mass violence in France, I can't help but to recall the words of Christ.

First, the French have, *rightly*, been taken to task for both their all too Islamic-friendly immigration policies and for acquiescing in the creation of intensely hostile Islamic enclaves— "No Go" zones. But it is sheer hypocrisy for such critics to castigate the French on these scores when America has been guilty of promoting its own version of Racially Correct-induced suicide over the span of the last nearly 50 years.

And the critics here are not innocent in this regard.

Since the mid-sixties, and *by design*, millions upon millions of mostly Third World Hispanics have been pouring into the United States. Republican politicians and their propagandists in the media labor inexhaustibly to convince the public that these immigrants are embodiments of "American conservative values" who, given enough time, will be ripe pickings for GOP votes.

In reality, by every social indicia—rates of illegitimacy, high school graduation, domestic abuse, drunken driving, *violent crime*, *gang-affiliation*, etc.—Hispanics fare substantially worse than whites and, in some areas, even slightly worse than blacks.

In some cities, like Los Angeles, Hispanics are *more likely* than blacks to belong to gangs.

Neither must we neglect to note that there is a not insignificant number of Hispanics residing in the states of the American Southwest who wish to reclaim them for Mexico.

Neighborhoods and entire cities in America have become "barrios" courtesy of the very same immigration policies that "conservative" critics of France's immigration policies, through a combination of ideological fantasizing and racial pandering, have only encouraged. While these barrios may not literally be the "No Go" zones of the Parisian suburbs, they *are* bastions of criminality and violence.

And they seem just as foreign to the rest of the country as the Muslim communities of France seem foreign to the rest of France: they are countries within countries.

Secondly, it's true that America, unlike France (and most of Europe), doesn't have an Islamic *immigration* problem. But there most definitely *is* an ever growing phenomenon of Islamic militancy in America, and it is occurring primarily among *black* Americans.

Much of the prison population in France consists of Muslims, and the prisons, in turn, serve as recruitment centers for Islamic jihadists. This, some commentators have remarked, poses big problems for France.

However, *America's* prison population consists of large numbers of Muslims as well. The difference, though, is that in America, Islamic convicts tend to be black and native to the country. But we rarely hear our "conservative" critics (much less anyone else) spending anytime talking about the problem that this poses to *our country*.

Yet a problem it is, for as recently as over the last few months, black American Muslims have murdered whites in the name of their religion. Right before Christmas, a black American

Muslim gunned down two NYPD officers as they sat harmlessly in their patrol car.

Thirdly, the Islamic element aside, in America, no more than *three percent* of the population—(mostly) young, black males—are responsible for nearly *50 percent* of all crime and *40 percent* of all violent crime.

Black neighborhoods and cities around the country are veritable war zones and economic wastelands. These black "ghettos" resemble in many ways the "ghettos" of France and other European lands.

They may not literally be "No Go" zones for police, but over the last half of a year since Ferguson (and, actually, long before that), we've seen the brutal treatment to which police, and sometimes fire fighters, are subjected upon entering our *de facto* No Go zones.

The *black* writer, Walter E. Williams, once said:

> *If we ignored inner-city violent crime, mostly committed by blacks and Hispanics, America would be a fairly civilized place.*

Where's the outrage? Too many "conservative" media spokespersons, along with their leftist counterparts, at least implicitly accept the narrative of White Oppression and Black Victimhood.

In the words of the black scholar, Shelby Steele, they suffer from "white guilt," an aching, perpetually present desire to "dissociate" themselves from their "racist" ancestors.

In truth, the brute and ugly fact of the matter is that for all their hollering about the need for courage in dealing with the threat of *Islam* (what they not so courageously, or honestly, insist upon calling "*Islamism*," "*Radical Islam*," "*Islamo-Fascism*," and other misleading terms), our so-called "conservative" media personalities are just *afraid*—so terribly afraid—to apply the same standards of morality to racial minorities as they apply to whites.

It seems to me that we should be *taking,* not *giving,* lessons in courage and political *in*correctness from the French.

And that's really saying something.

The Reality of Black-on-White Crime and Why It Must Be Discussed

As the nation remembers Martin Luther King's "I Have a Dream" speech, it should also note that while the self-appointed guardians of King's legacy, the "anti-racists," obsess over Paula Deen and liken Trayvon Martin to Emmet Till, they say *nothing* about interracial violence when it involves *black perpetrators* and *white victims.*

Below is a select list of interracial atrocities committed by blacks against whites. These forgotten victims are men and women, young and old.

Brad Heyka, Jason Befort, Aaron Sander, Heather Muller, "H.G.": In December of 2000, in Wichita, Kansas, over the course of hours, two brothers, Reginald and Jonathan Carr, robbed, beat, sexually tormented, and repeatedly raped three men and two women. They eventually shot all five victims, execution-style, in the backs of their heads before driving over their bodies with one of the victim's pick-up truck. "H.G." survived. Wearing nothing but a shirt, shot and battered, she walked a mile until she found help.

Channon Christian, Christopher Newsom: In 2007, this young couple was carjacked in Knoxville, Tennessee by four men and one woman. Both were raped—Newsom anally, Christian anally, vaginally, and orally. The former was shot and his body set on fire. The latter was suffocated over a span of hours inside of garbage bags—after she was forced to ingest bleach so as to remove traces of her assailants' DNA.

Sherry West, Antonio Santiago: On March 21 of this

year, this woman and her 13 month-old baby son were both shot while going for a walk in their Brunswick, Georgia neighborhood. The mother survived the bullets to her ear and leg. Little Antonio, however, died instantly when the bullet entered his face.

Joshua Heath Chellew: At the end of June, this 36 year-old man was attacked by four teenagers at a gas station outside of Atlanta, Georgia. In trying to escape the beating that he was suffering, Chellew was fatally struck by a passing car.

Jonathan Foster: On Christmas Eve, 2010, 12 year-old, Jonathan Foster was abducted from his home in Houston, Texas by a 44 year-old woman, Mona Nelson. The latter bound Foster and then murdered him with *a blowtorch*. She discarded his body in a ditch along the road where it was found four days later. Foster's remains were so badly charred that his corpse had to be identified by his dental records.

Delbert "Shorty" Benton: Just last week, the 89 year-old veteran of World War II was beaten to death by two teenagers armed with flashlights. Benton was making his way through the parking lot of one of the places that he regularly frequented when he was attacked.

Chris Lane: The 23 year-old Australian was in the States visiting his girlfriend. While on a run, some reportedly "bored" teenagers shot him in the back. Lane died shortly afterward. The thugs had a history of expressing hostility toward whites, and at least one of them was said by police to have laughed and danced upon being arrested.

Fannie Gumbinger: This 99 year-old Poughkeepsie, New York woman died last week when a 20 year-old burglar murdered her in her home. Police say she suffered "multiple injuries."

There is no shortage of people who will defend the deafening silence of the "anti-racists" with respect to these interracial horrors on the grounds that, supposedly, they had *nothing* to do with color. Black criminals seek out whites, it is often said, simply because whites are perceived as having more in the way of material goods.

Yet if this is true, then color or race most certainly *does* have something to do with these attacks: black criminals *profile* whites. But if there is nothing illegitimate about black predators (or others) profiling whites as "privileged," "advantaged," "racist," etc., then neither can it be said—as it is always said by "anti-racists"—that there is anything illegitimate about whites profiling blacks.

Only hypocrisy, illogic, or some combination of the two could make one suggest otherwise.

Another common criticism centers on the alleged irrelevance of the race of perpetrators and victims. After all, it is *the murder* that should be condemned; the color of murderer and murdered of no consequence.

Ah. So, if this is the case, then "racism" should never come under attack at all, for it isn't, say, the color of the Klansmen and the black victims that they lynched that is blameworthy, but *the lynching* itself.

There isn't a single "anti-racist" who would dream to reason thus.

One reason that black-on-white violence should be discussed is that it is both ubiquitous and evil. The blacks responsible for it constitute but a tiny percentage of the national population, and yet they are several times more likely than their white counterparts to engage in interracial violence.

Another reason that black-on-white cruelty must be brought out into the open is that it is a reality that can only weaken the false narrative of unrelenting White Oppression and perpetual Black Suffering that has been used by demagogues and opportunists to prop up the destructive policies that they've promoted *in the name* of combating "racism."

Jack Kerwick

The Ideology of Blackism

Over the span of the last four years, there has been much talk over whether or not our 44th president is a socialist. Of course, that Barack Obama is a socialist will be denied only by those who choose to give his redistributionist agenda a different name. But looking back at the final weeks that lead up to the 2012 Election Day, we should have realized that Obama was committed to another ideology, one that hasn't been nearly as often remarked upon.

Obama, you see, is every bit as much a proponent of *blackism* as he is a champion of socialism. In fact, it is his embrace of the former that explains his embrace of the latter.

Like any other ideology, blackism consists of a small handful of basic, interrelated principles.

First, the blackist affirms an explicitly—and thoroughly—racial conception of history.

Historical actors, here, are nothing more or less than abstract racial categories—whites, blacks, etc. And history is an epic melodrama, a perpetual contest between the forces of white "racism" or "supremacy," on the one hand, and, on the other, the "oppression" suffered by people of color.

Second, white racism is endemic. This the blackist must believe with all of his heart. Whatever gains black Americans and formerly colonized peoples of color in other parts of the world have made over the decades, white racism remains as formidable, and destructive, a force as it has ever been. This explains the blackist's insistence that white racism, far from diminishing, has simply gone covert.

Third, blackism demands of all of its adherents in good standing that, whenever possible, they express some measure of indignation or rage regarding the historical injustices suffered by blacks and the persistent omnipresence of—what else?—white racism.

103

Fourth, the blackist unabashedly heeds the call of "social" or "racial justice." What this in turn means is that he must favor a robust and activist government, for only such a government will possess the power necessary to compensate blacks for the past harms that had been visited upon them by white racism. And only such a government will be strong enough to protect them against its ravages in the present and future.

Finally, central to blackism is the idea of "racial authenticity." Racial authenticity can be achieved, it promises, by way of the very simple act of affirming blackism!

Like all ideologies, the ideology of blackism is a distillation of what we may call "black culture." It is the Cliff Note, so to speak, the *Reader's Digest* version, of a complex of black cultural traditions stretching back centuries.

In theory, the tenets of blackism can be affirmed by anyone. However, only a biologically black person can be a blackist.

That is, it is instant made for just those blacks like Barack Obama who, while biologically black, know next to nothing about black culture. For those blacks, like Obama, who are in search of racial authenticity, the ideology of blackism is their Rosetta stone. It is their salvation. The reason for this is simple.

To genuinely know a tradition well enough to make it one's own, it is necessary to immerse oneself in it.

In glaring contrast, the knowledge of an ideology can be mastered by anyone in no time at all, for an ideology is constituted by just a few simple propositions that any school child can effortlessly confine to memory.

The blackist par excellence was, not coincidentally, the one person whose autobiography Obama alludes to more than any other book in his first memoir: Malcolm X.

Malcolm would invoke "the authority of history," as he put it, in condemning whites for having "stole our fathers and mothers from their culture of silk and satins" and bringing "them to this land in the belly of a ship [.]" He famously declared that blacks "didn't land on Plymouth Rock," but "Plymouth Rock landed" on blacks.

Malcolm also blasted whites for having secured their "position of leadership in the world" through "conquering, killing, exploiting, pillaging, raping, bullying" and "beating." Throughout the white man's "entire advance through history, he has been waving the banner of Christianity" in the one hand and, in the other, "the sword and the flintlock," Malcolm charged.

The light-complexioned Malcolm, who, like Obama, was raised and schooled within a predominantly white environment, never spared an occasion to assert his racial authenticity. In addition to decrying white racism from the rooftops, he was also fond of blasting other blacks—like Martin Luther King, Booker Washington, Jackie Robinson, Joe Louis, and Roy Wilkins—as "Uncle Toms."

Obama, obviously, is not of the same temperament as Malcolm. But he is every bit as much of a blackist.

That, as its subtitle makes abundantly clear, his first memoir was designed to be "a story of *race,*" weighs substantially in favor of this thesis. But if this doesn't convince, there is much more evidence ready at hand.

Obama has a long history of allying himself with the most radical and anti-American of types, it is true. But it is his 20-plus year relationship with his pastor and friend, the self-avowed champion of Black Liberation Theology and Louis Farrakhan admirer, Jeremiah Wright, which most decisively determines his allegiance to blackism.

Yet now that Obama has had four years to govern, we can see that he hasn't governed in a manner that is appreciably different from that which we could expect from Wright himself.

As Pat Buchanan and other commentators have noted, Obama's redistributionist policies have the effect of disproportionately benefitting blacks while disproportionately harming those whites whose resources will be confiscated to fund these policies.

Obama has uttered not a word to stop his supporters from charging his opponents with racism. He has actually exacerbated interracial relations by siding with those blacks, like Trayvon Martin and Henry Louis Gates, who were involved in nationally publicized confrontations with whites. Flash mobs have formed all across the country during Obama's tenure, yet he has been silent in the face of these orgies of black-on-white violence.

His appointments, from Eric Holder to Van Jones, further reveal Obama's racial commitments.

Going into the voting booth on November 6, let us realize that while our current president is an ideologue, the ideology to which he is most attached—and that is most dangerous—is not socialism or leftism.

It is blackism.

Another Travesty of Justice: The Carr Brothers Live

In December of 2000, within the span of less than a week, two brothers, Reginald and Jonathan Carr, engaged in a series of crimes in Wichita that Kansans recognize as among the worst in their state's history.

First, they abducted and robbed assistant baseball coach Andrew Schreiber. Three days later, the Carrs set their sights upon 55 year-old librarian and cellist, Ann Walenta: they shot and killed Walenta as she attempted to flee them in her automobile.

But it wasn't until three days after *this* murder that the Carrs' campaign of evil reached its horrifying climax.

On the night of December 14, the Carrs broke into the residence of Brad Heyka, Aaron Sander, and Jason Befort. Heyka was a financial analyst, Sander a seminary student preparing for the priesthood, and Befort a high school science teacher and coach.

Also in the home that evening were Heather Muller, Sander's former girlfriend and a graduate student who also happened to work as a pre-school teacher at a local church, and a young woman named "H.G."—a school teacher to whom Befort was about to propose and who would be the sole survivor of the grisly events that were about to unfold over the next few hours.

Armed with guns, the Carrs made their victims perform sexual acts on *one another*. The women were forced to penetrate each other's vaginas orally and digitally, and the men were forced to have sex with the women. Yet when the Carrs discovered that Befort and "H.G." were romantically involved, they *prevented* them from having sexual intercourse with one another, choosing instead to force Befort watch as they coerced his friends to essentially rape his fiancée to be.

At one point, when Aaron Sander couldn't get an erection, the Carrs put a gun to his head and threatened to shoot him lest his momentary dysfunction resolve itself within the two minute time frame that they allotted him. When the time expired, the Carrs returned Sander to the closet in which they corralled their prey with "H.G." and retrieved Befort and Heyka, both of whom were then forced to sexually assault Heather Muller, whose pain-racked groans, "H.G." later testified, were all too audible from the next room.

The sexual degradation that the Carrs inflicted upon their victims was punctured by episodic beatings that the Carrs gave the men—beatings that appear to have involved the use of golf clubs. It was also interrupted by drives to ATM machines where the Carrs had their victims withdraw funds.

Yet the Carr brothers themselves also repeatedly raped, vaginally and orally, the two women.

About three hours into this nightmare, the Carrs drove their victims to a snow-covered field. The men were stuffed into the trunk of Sander's Honda Accord that Jonathan Carr drove while Reginald drove Befort's truck. Being less than 20 degrees, the air was frigid—and yet their captors permitted Befort, Heyka, and Sander to wear not a single article of clothing, while permitting Muller and "H.G." to wear only a sweater.

Once they arrived at their destination, the Carrs commanded their prey to kneel in the snow and ice. As the five begged for their lives, their tormentors shot them each in the backs of their heads. Then, they drove over their bodies with Befort's truck.

Miraculously, courtesy of a metal *hairclip,* "H.G." survived. She didn't even lose consciousness. Instead, she tried to help her boyfriend, from whom "blood was squirting everywhere"—including from his eyes—by wrapping around his head her sweater, the only article of clothing, mind you, that she was wearing.

Naked, she walked over a mile in the freezing cold to a stranger's home in search of help for herself and her friends—for whom, sadly, it was already too late.

Meanwhile, the Carrs would return to their victims' home to pillage it. While there, they encountered Nikki, the dog that belonged to "H.G." The Carrs pummeled the poor animal with a golf club before driving an ice pick through it.

The Carrs were arrested and went to trial. "H.G." took the stand, explaining that she constantly awakes in "cold sweats" from her "nightmares," that "every morning" she must "carefully blow-dry" her hair to "cover up the spot that," as result of being shot, "can no longer grow hair," and that she has "the scars" on her knees from the rapes to which these "two soulless monsters" subjected her.

"H.G." also testified that she has a sexually-transmitted disease courtesy of one of her rapists.

That a jury of their peers convicted the Carrs of capital murder and sentenced them to death suggests that they agreed with "H.G." that her attackers *are* "soulless monsters." Yet on Friday, July 25, by a 6-1 decision, the Kansas Supreme Court, citing *procedural* problems, maintained the convictions while *overturning* the Carrs' death sentences.

According to *The Topeka Capital-Journal,* Republican members of the GOP-controlled Legislature have complained about the "'activist' streak" of the justices while noting that Kansas hasn't had an execution since 1965. But while an anti-death penalty sentiment may account for this outrage, that racial considerations may be in play is also a possibility not to be overlooked.

The brothers Carr, you see, are *black. All* of their victims are *white.*

Can there be any doubt that had the racial roles here been reversed that everything from the coverage of this case—which, nationally speaking, has been virtually zilch—to this latest travesty of justice would be different?

In any event, Reginald and Jonathan Carr are as guilty as sin itself of raw savagery. There can be no conceivable justification for permitting their natural existence another moment.

And there can be no conceivable justification for nominating judges who allow their racial preoccupations and other political predilections to prevail over their duty to rule justly.

Lies Surrounding the Central Park Jogger Outrage

Twenty-five years ago, Trisha Meili—"the Central Park jogger"— was a 28 year-old employee for a prestigious Manhattan investment banker when she was mercilessly beaten, raped, and left for dead by thugs.

Meili lost approximately *80 percent* of her blood. Her skull was fractured to the point that her one eye had popped out of its socket. On the scale of 3 to 15 that neurologists use to gauge brain functioning, Meili's was assigned a rating of 4. She spent nearly the next two weeks in a coma, with experts expecting her to die.

This crime became a racially explosive issue, for Meili was

white and her assailants were not: Of the 30 or so minority youths that had been randomly terrorizing park dwellers, four blacks and one Hispanic confessed to having engaged in the attack on Meili. Antron McCray, Kevin Richardson, Raymond Santana, Kharey Wise, and Yusef Salaam were arrested, tried, convicted, and issued prison sentences.

But in 2002, long after "the Central Park Five," as documentarian and apologist for the convicts, Ken Burns has dubbed them, had done their time, and long after *the statute of limitations* on the 13 year-old crime *had expired*, convicted serial rapist and murderer, Matias Reyes, who was already serving a life term, confessed to being Meili's lone assailant. DNA testing confirmed that it was Matias' semen—and his alone—that was found on Meili's body and around the scene of the crime.

Shortly afterwards, District Attorney Robert Morgenthau prevailed upon his state's Supreme Court to "vacate" the convictions of "the Central Park Five." Not unsurprisingly, the latter sued the City of New York for wrongful imprisonment to the tune of *$250 million*.

In June, courtesy of the ever illustrious Mayor DiBlasio, "the Central Park Five" discovered that they would receive *$40 million*.

Not since the O.J. Simpson acquittal have we witnessed this gross a travesty of justice. Yet it's also a travesty of intelligence, for only a fool—or perhaps a liar—could think that "the Central Park Five" were innocent of *anything*, much less the attack on Trisha Meili.

For starters, no one has ever disputed that the Harlem thugs had been in Central Park that fateful evening for the sole purpose of assaulting and mugging innocents (one of whom had been bludgeoned with a pipe). As is the wont of cowards, "the Five" set upon only those who they outnumbered, those who were weaker and more vulnerable. This they confessed from the moment they were in police custody.

To the present day, they have never retracted *this* confession.

Yet "the Five" also proceeded immediately to implicate themselves in the assault on *Meili*. On *multiple* occasions, while alone with the police *as well as* when they were accompanied by their adult relatives, they left no doubts about their role in this act of barbarism:

Antron McCray:

> *We charged her. We got her on the ground. Everybody started hitting her and stuff. She was on the ground. Everybody stompin' and everything. Then we got, each—I grabbed one arm, some other kid grabbed one arm, and we grabbed her legs and stuff. Then we all took turns getting on her, getting on top of her.*

Kevin Richardson:

> *Raymond [Santana] had her arms, and Steve [Lopez] had her legs. He spread it out. And Antron [McCray] got on top, took her panties off.*

Raymond Santana:

> *He was smackin' her, he was sayin', 'Shut up, bitch!' Just smackin' her...I was grabbin' the lady's tits.*

Kharey Wise:

> *This was my first rape.*

Ann Coulter reminds us that Melody Jackson, whose brother was friends with Wise, *testified* that the latter told her by phone while he was incarcerated at Riker's Island that even though *he* didn't actually rape Meili, he *did* restrain the victim's legs while Kevin Richardson "fucked her."

Jackson, incidentally, informed the police of this exchange only because she thought that it would *help* Wise's case.

Coulter also notes that one of the youths apprehended by police shortly after the attack against Meili insisted—*prior to being questioned*—that he knew "who did the *murder*." This is proof that, at the very least, the pummeling that Meili endured was witnessed by multiple people *and* that its severity was such that it was assumed that it was fatal.

Meili *was* left for dead.

But there is more.

This same punk—again, mind you, without even being asked about the attack, much less a murder—fingered none other than *Antron McCray* as "the murderer."

Multiple videotaped confessions of "the Five"; the presence of semen, blood, and hair on all of the suspects; a scratch on Kevin Richardson's neck that, *in the company of his father,* he admitted he received by Meili; and several witness accounts confirmed for the police that the vermin who Ken Burns would years later make into martyrs were as guilty as sin itself of initiating and facilitating an attack against Trisha Meili that nearly cost the poor woman her life.

Matias Reyes semen was the only attacker's DNA found *on* Meili or at the crime scene.

However, neither this nor the word of this serial rapist and murderer that he acted alone goes any distance whatsoever toward proving the innocence of "the Central Park Five."

Police have been prevented by the District Attorney, Robert Morgenthau, who recommended that the convictions of "the Five" be vacated, from interrogating Reyes.

Linda Fairstein, the original prosecutor in this case, expressed her certainty that "the Central Park Five" are guilty. Reyes, she believes, merely finished what they had started. As for this notion that the NYPD "coerced" false confessions from the suspects, Mike Sheehan, one of the central detectives who investigated the crime, and who, in his own words, had spent decades taking "over 1,000 confessions, in 3,000 homicides," has nothing but contempt.

"All of this stuff about coercion really pisses me off," Sheehan has said. "Do you honestly think that we—detectives with more than 20 years in, family men with pensions—would risk all of that so we could put words in the mouth of a 15 year-old kid? Absolutely not."

Even Morgenthau concedes that no police misconduct—like coercing the teens into admitting to a crime in which they had zero involvement—ever occurred.

Now "the Central Park Five" is $40 million richer.

But the taxpayers of New York City—including the victims of the "wilding" rampage visited upon Central Park 25 years ago—have suffered a loss far greater than this.

For that matter, the fortune of "the Central Park Five" is the misfortune of all decent people.

Thoughts on the Shooting Death of Michael Brown

To the proliferation of articles on the shooting death of black Missourian Michael Brown via white police officer, Darren Wilson, I register the following considerations.

Firstly, at this time when black underclass thugs are ruining the quality of life in but another once-decent town while their black and white media spokespersons bellyache over the unrelenting racial oppression to which black Americans are supposedly subject, let us call to mind all of the rosy promises made six years ago when Barack Hussein Obama first set his sights on the presidency.

Pundits both black and white, Democrat and Republican,

113

assured us that the election of a black man with an Islamic-sounding name was sure to endear America to Muslims around the globe while ushering in a "post-racial" era here at home. Remember that?

The Islamic world, always a cauldron of violence, is even more violent, more emboldened now than it has been in the past. Something similar can be said for the world of black America, or at least black *urban* America—as the current happenings in Ferguson, Missouri painfully reveal.

Secondly, those "conservative" commentators who claim to be agnostic on whether Darren Wilson, in the absence of any provocation on the part of Michael Brown, killed the latter solely for thrills imply that they're open to the possibility that *this actually could have happened*.

In other words, they *legitimize* the outrageous notion that white police officers routinely seek out unsuspecting, law-abiding black citizens to gun down.

I'll say it now: while, admittedly, I do not know the details of what actually transpired between Wilson and Brown, I most certainly *do* know—and so, too, I'm ready to bet, does every other commentator who isn't an anti-white, anti-police ideologue—that Officer Wilson is *not* guilty of any of the charges that the black criminals in Ferguson and their apologists in Washington D.C. and the media are leveling against him.

Wilson is a decorated police officer. Brown was a thug who just moments prior to his fatal encounter with Wilson had been captured on video surveillance engaging in a strong-arm robbery of a convenience store.

This is one reason why my I'm strongly disposed to sympathize with Wilson's and the Ferguson Police Department's account of events over that supplied by Dorian Johnson, the 22 year-old who was with Brown when he was killed—and who served as his accomplice to the robbery and assault of a clerk.

But there is another reason why I believe Wilson acted

justifiably. And this brings me to my third piece of food for thought:

We have heard this story before.

Last summer, it was the Trayvon Martin shooting death that had the agents of the "Racism-Industrial-Complex" (RIC) in the media in a tizzy.

Presumably, genuinely *white* "racists" were slim pickings. Thus, they invented one by turning the clearly Latino-looking George Zimmerman into a "white Hispanic." At the same time, these same activists substituted for the unflattering portrait of the real Trayvon Martin a disinfected one that was more friendly to their template of white oppression and black victimhood—the same template through which they are now filtering the incident in Ferguson.

And like in the case of Martin, RIC agents would have us rather see their sanitized depiction of Michael Brown—the bright-eyed, college bound "gentle giant"—than the hulking man whose audacity and recklessness were as large as his physical stature, the punk who thought nothing of either depriving another man of his hard earned property or assaulting him when his victim resisted.

A bad actor is one who makes it obvious that he or she is *trying* to act. Similarly, in "miscasting" the most unlikely types into the roles that they've written, it's *obvious,* painfully obvious, that the Al Sharptons of the world are trying to sell us a bill of goods.

Fourth, that the shameful violence and crime—the "rioting"—that's occurring in Ferguson and the insidious rhetoric from which it arose have absolutely *nothing* to do with a desire for justice or interracial peace can be gotten all too easily from the deafening *silence* with which the shocking rate and nature of *black-on-white* violence is invariably met.

For instance, recently in Iowa, a white 97 year-old veteran of World War II—Rupert "Andy" Anderson—and his 94 year-old wife of many years were bludgeoned with a pipe courtesy of a black Ethiopian immigrant. Mrs. Anderson, though bloodied, survived this attack that occurred in her home. Her husband, however, wasn't so fortunate.

Whether it's this case or any other number of grisly instances of black-on-white violence, when the media decides to cover it at all, they invariably either avoid or deny the racial dynamic. In writing about the Anderson murder, journalist Nicholas Stix refers to this phenomenon as the "preemptive MSM [Main Stream Media] propaganda template [.]"

Finally, while it is verboten to raise this question in "respectable" (i.e. Politically Correct) company, raise it we must: If things are really as terrible—as "racist"—in America as so many blacks in Ferguson and elsewhere would have us believe, then why aren't these same blacks demanding—not *requesting,* but *demanding*—that blacks be granted their own separate homeland? We're not necessarily talking about a "back-to-Africa" movement, but perhaps a country carved out of American land?

After all, today, when blacks demand something, anything— or when they're demanding it from *whites*—they usually get it. At any rate, blacks, or at least black "leaders," have zero reluctance about expressing their demands.

And wouldn't it be infinitely better for everyone to peacefully go our separate ways rather than perpetually be at each other's throats?

That not a single black "leader," or anyone else, for that matter, has so much as suggested this as a possibility, much less demanded it, speaks volumes.

Racial Irrationality in Ferguson

Thomas Sowell once noted that few topics so tap the irrational excesses of a person's intellect as that of race. At the very least, contemporary race-related discussions are almost invariably ridden with irrationality.

The issue of Ferguson, Missouri is but the latest exhibition of this all too pervasive phenomenon.

Yet, to be sure, it isn't just the usual suspects on the recognizable left—the obvious racialist and socialist ideologues—that have revealed just how dangerously shallow, both intellectually and morally, they can be on this racially-charged front.

Some neoconservative and libertarian commentators are also guilty on this score.

First, in order to sound "objective"—and, truth be told, not *all that* politically *in*correct—neoconservative commentators continually caution against judging hastily: since we weren't there, they say, we should remain agnostic on the question regarding the guilt or innocence of Officer Darren Wilson (the officer who the black rioters in Ferguson and their apologists in the media say *murdered* Michael Brown).

In taking this line, however, these same commentators actually *legitimize* the notion that, in 2014, there are white police officers who routinely patrol the streets in search of young black teenagers to gun down in cold blood.

Give me a break.

We know enough now—if we didn't know enough when word of this story first broke—that, at a minimum, there was *no* murder that took place here.

Second, we're hearing quite a bit about "the militarization" of the police in Ferguson, and how it is *this,* and not the riotous conduct of the black citizens of that city and the incendiary rhetoric of their self-avowed "leaders, that is responsible, or largely responsible, for the undermining of civilization that is transpiring there.

National Review writer Kevin Williamson is one person busily advancing this line. Some libertarian writers at Lewrockwell.com are (predictably) doing so as well.

It's rubbish, but another transparent, and transparently pathetic, attempt to excavate some "root cause" to account for black dysfunction. The idea that the presence of "militarized" police is somehow responsible for the exhibitions of barbarism that have unfolded in Ferguson is of a logical piece with the old, tired mantra that poverty causes crime.

But as Walter E. Williams once remarked, while there certainly is a causal relation between poverty and crime, it runs in exactly the opposite direction of that imagined by the conventional wisdom: crime *causes* poverty.

Similarly, the police in Ferguson are "militarized" precisely *because of* the legions of merciless black rioters with whom they have to contend.

Yet there's another consideration that gives up the lie that the police in Ferguson have provoked the black violence there: sixty-seven percent black Ferguson, like heavily populated black areas throughout the country, was ridden with crime and violence long before anyone ever heard of Michael Brown.

Most of this criminality, though, consists of black-on-black attacks.

Is the militarization of the Ferguson police responsible for the obscene rates and grisly nature of the crime that has been everyday life in Ferguson for years? Is it this that explains why blacks are murdering, raping, beating, and pillaging other blacks?

Is the "militarization" of police in Detroit, Chicago, Atlanta, Camden, Newark, the Bronx, Los Angeles and black cities throughout the nation the cause of the truly scandalous degree of violence and vice that's become a permanent fixture of daily existence for the residents of these areas?

At long last, let's be truthful: police officers in high crime areas—which, today, is *virtually* synonymous with high *black* areas—*must* be armed to the teeth to protect themselves *as well as* the law-abiding citizens of these areas who are routinely victimized by the predators in their midst.

Rand Paul—who, *at one time*, I was strongly disposed to support—has recently made shameful comments concerning the shameful goings-on in Ferguson. "Given the racial disparities in our criminal justice system," Paul said, "it is impossible for African-Americans not to feel like their government is particularly targeting them."

To judge from this sentence, one could be forgiven for thinking that "the government" arbitrarily arrests, tries, convicts, and sentences (or executes) a wildly disproportionate number of blacks over whites (and Hispanics, and Indians, and Asians, etc.).

Again, what we witness in this piece of unreason is causal confusion run amok: There is a stronger "government" (police) presence in black communities *because* blacks are wildly overrepresented among criminals.

Or, if you will, "the government"—the police—is doing exactly what it should be doing in "targeting," not "African-Americans," but *criminals*—many, all too many, of whom are black.

Let's see: For six years, we've had a black president, a person, remember, who blacks and whites, Democrats and some Republicans, assured us was going to usher in a post-racial era. We also have a black Attorney General. The government at the most powerful levels, in other words, is run by black men.

And yet, according to Rand Paul, it is reasonable for blacks to suspect that their government is targeting them?

Sowell has never been more right: nothing screams "irrational" like contemporary talk over race relations.

The Root Causes of America's Fergusons

Ferguson, Missouri now stands as a microcosmic expression of black America. It seems that partisans of all stripes turn to Ferguson and, without missing a beat, boil down the staggering battery of problems plaguing "the black community" to a *single* cause.

Neoconservative Republicans invariably attribute the rampant dysfunction of lower and underclass blacks to life under the control of the Democrat party. The usual suspects on the left can be counted upon to pin all of the seemingly insurmountable challenges facing blacks to—what else?—"racism!"

Libertarians, or at least libertarians of a certain ideological flavor, reserve scarcely a word of condemnation, if that, for black purveyors of violence, choosing instead to account for this violence in terms of "police brutality" or "the militarization" of police.

So, both neoconservatives and libertarians, politically, are determinists. When it comes to black pathology, the government is the devil.

And then there are white "race realists" who are convinced that the astronomical rates of crime, violence, illegitimacy, etc. that mark black communities throughout the country stem from the *genetics* of blacks themselves.

According to this line, since the average black IQ is lower than the average white IQ, blacks, on average, have shorter time horizons, less impulse control, and so forth. These genetic disadvantages, in turn, dispose them to engage in the sort of conduct on exhibit in Ferguson at the present moment.

There are two points that need to be made here.

First, all four of these explanations of black pathology bear more similarities to one another than their adherents would care to admit.

For starters, they are alike forms of *reductionism*. And they are alike exceedingly—which is to say, unreasonably—*simplistic* forms of reductionism.

Moreover, race realists may or may not realize this, but their genetics-centered theory of the Fergusons of the world no more holds blacks culpable for their actions than do those theories advanced by neoconservatives, libertarians, and leftists: Within the framework of any of these models, blacks are exempted from *all* responsibility.

And this, of course, means that blacks are divested of their personhood, their moral agency.

Persons are subjects whose conduct is freely chosen in accordance with reasons. In stark contrast, objects are things whose behavior is determined by causes.

If it is to any of the forgoing explanations of black conduct that we must turn to understand the actions of, say, the rioters in Ferguson, then, paradoxically, there is no *conduct* here to be explained: the black rioters are no different from any other material objects whose *behavior* is to be understood solely in reference to the great law of cause and effect.

This is one problem—I think it is fatal—from which all *scientific* accounts of human conduct suffer: they *are* scientific.

And even if they are only pseudo-scientific—some people would say that all of the "social sciences" fit this description—that they insist upon speaking *the language* of science in accounting for *moral* conduct is enough to convict them of an incorrigible *confusion* of *categories*: the vocabulary of morality and that of science are not only mutually *incompatible;* they are mutually *incommensurable.*

And this just means that the terms pertaining to the one category defy *translation* into the terms of the other.

Beside this, though, they just don't work.

"Racism" has long served as a catch-all term that means virtually nothing. And it means nothing because it means whatever the person who happens to be using it at the moment wants for it to mean.

In any event, it is as profoundly idiotic as it is offensive to suggest that the violence and destruction that are features of everyday life for underclass black communities throughout the country are a function of the fact that white people don't like them (if *this* is what we take "racism" to mean).

121

And neither the Democratic Party nor Big Government ("Statism") generally can account for the glaring dysfunctions of ghetto existence.

The Democratic Party presides over some of the most affluent, low-crime areas of the country, places like San Francisco and all of New England, for instance. And Big Government is a fact of life for *all* Americans—yet, thank God, America is *not* Ferguson or Detroit.

That these three paradigms serve the purpose of exempting blacks of responsibility for their actions explains their value. Think about it: when was the last time you heard any of their proponents address, say, black rioters with so much as a fraction of the sternness that they reserve for reproaching their own children for misconduct that isn't nearly as egregious as that on display in Ferguson?

It doesn't happen.

But the genetics-based account of black conduct divests blacks of moral responsibility as well.

While genetics certainly determine, to some extent, all sorts of things, including intelligence, and while individuals and groups do indeed differ in all sorts of respects, including intelligence, the genetics-grounded theory of black criminality of the sort that makes the Ghetto the Ghetto is unconvincing.

When we look back throughout the history of our own country alone, we see that it has had more than its share of "Fergusons," the vast majority of which, up until the first half of the 20th century, have been perpetrated *by whites.*

It may surprise most people, black, white, and other, to hear this, but it is true all of the same.

The Racism-Industrial-Complex and Ferguson

Justice was served in Ferguson, Missouri.

Some thoughts:

First, the usual suspects in the leftist media and their heroes in the White House and in the Department of Justice were once again as wrong as can be. This is wholly unsurprising given their investment in "the Myth of the Hobbled Black," as one black commentator described it.

This fiction is the thread that binds Big Government, Big Academia, Big Business, and Big Media into one colossal industry, what we can call the *Racism-Industrial-Complex* (RIC).

In all sorts of ways—emotionally, psychologically, monetarily, and politically—RIC agents profit immeasurably from promoting the line of endemic white "racism" and black suffering. Thus, they scarcely if ever address the astronomical rate and ghastly nature of black-on-white crime while sparing no opportunity to invent white villains—even when they have to transform a Hispanic (George Zimmerman) into one.

And this brings us to our next point:

Aliens from another galaxy who have just landed on planet Earth could be forgiven for thinking that perhaps Michael Brown really was gunned down in cold blood by a foaming-at-the-mouth "racist" cop who had been on the hunt for any innocent black person that he could find.

Americans, at least those of us who have been alive for more than a few years and who don't have an ideological axe to grind, have no such excuse for entertaining any such suspicions. There are some very simple reasons for this.

For starters, *we have seen this story before.* Back in August, when the rest of the world became aware of Ferguson, I reminded readers of this column that Michael Brown and Darren Wilson are characters with whom Americans have long been familiar. Whenever a black person gets the short end of the stick in a confrontation with white people, RIC agents in the media and elsewhere immediately impose upon events the impress of their template of choice: the Myth of White Oppression and Black Victimization.

Yet, virtually to an incident, they wind up with egg on their faces as facts surface and reality sends their fantasies soaring to the ground.

This is why some of us knew that Michael Brown was Tawana Brawley, the Duke Lacrosse Fake Rape victim, the Central Park Five, and Trayvon Martin by another name.

And it's why *everyone* with a modicum of experience with American race relations and a semblance of reason should've known the same.

Secondly, just moments before he was killed, Michael Brown was captured *on video* engaging in a strong-arm robbery of a business owner half his size. Darren Wilson, in sharp contrast, was a decorated police officer. That the former was the bad guy and the latter the good guy should have been a no-brainer to anyone who values decency.

Thirdly, if white police officers (or any other whites) are really that determined to slaughter innocent blacks, then why wouldn't they just set up shop outside of black churches throughout America and pickoff churchgoers? After all, isn't the image of a burning black church (along with that of the noose) just the image of white racial hatred that the media has busily promoted?

Furthermore, if white cops (and other whites) hate blacks indiscriminately, then *why would they* insist upon risking their lives on the most dangerous streets in America where they would be forced to deal mostly with *young men* who are *armed*? Why *not* lay in wait of blacks of every demographic group in an environment—like the grounds of a church—that is safe?

White police officers have their run-ins with just those blacks—young and male—responsible for the overwhelming majority of *crime* within black communities. This same demographic is responsible for a disproportionately large share of crime throughout the nation.

Finally, the truth is that white police officers obviously do *not* have it in for blacks. In fact, even when it comes to black low life thugs of the type that have descended upon Ferguson, the last thing white police officers want are fatal confrontations, for everyone knows that evidence, law, and common sense be damned, the shooting death of even the most repulsive of black criminals via a white cop is likely to erupt into Ferguson-style riots.

One last thought: ironically, it is the *reaction* to the grand jury's brave decision to not indict Officer Wilson that *vindicates* him and every other police officer in Ferguson—and in the many, many Fergusons throughout America. The godless actions of the evil doers in Ferguson that Americans have had the great misfortune of viewing from the comfort of their living rooms reveal the war-like conditions in which police officers must labor in inner cities across the land.

Five Racial Double Standards

In Florida, a 13 year-old white boy is savagely beaten on a school bus by three black thugs. Yet it gains not a fraction of the attention paid by the press of the whole Western world to Oprah Winfrey's claims to have fallen prey to "racism" while perusing a fancy boutique in Switzerland.

The racial double standards accentuated by the juxtaposition of these two events couldn't be more glaring.

Winfrey is a billionaire, one of the wealthiest, most famous, and, to the extent that she's done more than rub elbows with the biggest names in Hollywood and American politics, one of the most influential human beings on the planet. If anyone qualifies as "*privileged*," to use the left's lingo, it is Winfrey.

The Florida boy who was beaten senseless, like the shop clerk whom Winfrey accused of "racism," is an obscure figure of modest means. Again, parroting the left, he is among the "powerless" or "voiceless."

The racially-oriented cruelty to which Winfrey's allegedly been subjected consists in her having been denied the opportunity to inspect a nearly $40,000.00 pocketbook.

The cruelty to which the 13 year-old from Florida was subjected is a vicious beating by three black cowards.

Within the last couple of days, Winfrey's "victimizer" has staunchly rejected her accusation. Immediately thereafter, Winfrey began backpedaling, going even so far as to apologize for all of the attention that this incident has received.

Winfrey, you see, was less than fully truthful, if she wasn't outright dishonest, about her treatment at the proverbial hands of the white shop clerk in Switzerland.

The 13 year-old, however, *really* did suffer at the literal hands of his assailants: he was beaten mercilessly and then *robbed*. The incident was caught on video and his tormentors have confessed to the charges against them.

Still, Winfrey's non-incident throws the world off of its axis while the plight of this poor 13 year-old is neglected. The media rushes to elicit sympathy—and *guilt*—for another alleged black victim, even if she happens to be among the most fortunate human beings to have ever lived, and even if the "indignity" to which she was supposedly subjected is not exactly the stuff of which the annals of human suffering are filled.

At the same time, the media rushes just as quickly to suppress the deeds of black victimizers—even when they engage in acts of sheer barbarity.

Moving beyond these two events, there seems to be no end to the racial double standards.

First, loudly and proudly, we're all supposed to decry racial discrimination when the discriminators are white and those discriminated against are black. To do otherwise is to betray one's "racism."

However, unless one loudly and proudly *endorses* so-called "affirmative action"—racial discrimination *in favor of* blacks—one is "racist."

So, the "racist" is he who seeks to place blacks at a disadvantage with respect to whites. No less of a "racist" is the person who refuses to give blacks an *advantage* over whites.

Second, it is "racist" for a white person to render judgments about "black America" on the bases of the actions of individual blacks. This explains why, say, "racial profiling" is held by the professional "anti-racists" to be morally obscene.

Yet it is *not* "racist" for blacks (and whites) to complain endlessly about the transgressions of "*white* America." Very few white Americans—including Southerners—owned slaves or had anything but contempt for those whites, like the men who beat and murdered poor Emmet Till, who aspired to treat blacks cruelly. Moreover, if not for the gallant efforts of legions of white Americans, the injustices of the past would be the injustices of the present.

And yet whites are judged collectively while blacks are freed of such an oppressive restraint.

Third, when whites flee those areas that lower and underclass blacks begin to inhabit, it is called "white flight" and chalked up to "racism." But when *blacks* do the same, it is called "movin' on up" and applauded. Though as John Perazzo noted in *The Myths that Divide Us,* at least as many blacks fled the chronic dysfunction of the black underclass in the 1980's and beyond as did whites in preceding decades.

Fourth, for the scandalous rate of criminality and violence among blacks, young black men in particular, an explanation in "root causes" is always sought out. Yet "root causes" are never, ever invoked when it comes to accounting for "white racism." It is understandable, even justifiable, that blacks should harbor a violent, even murderous, rage toward whites for centuries of oppression. But that whites may be wary of blacks is chalked up as the species of some raw, uncaused prejudice.

Finally, blacks commit a vastly larger share of interracial

crime than that perpetrated by whites.

Relatively rarely are they charged with "hate" crimes. For example, five black guttersnipes in Knoxville, Tennessee carjack, abduct, rape, torture, and murder a young white couple, but because some of the assailants had white girlfriends and because, as far as could be determined, none of them had used any racial epithets in connection with their victims, race is deemed not to have played any role whatsoever in this outrage.

Every effort is made to discern *the intentions* of black perpetrators.

Such is not the case when it comes to whites.

According to the doctrine of "institutional racism," white *society* is incorrigibly "racist"—even if white *individuals* have *the best of intentions.* More exactly, even if whites are *consciously* well meaning toward blacks, *subconsciously* they entertain the most degrading of stereotypes concerning them.

There are more racial double standards that could be listed. Space precludes it here. Still, these five are plenty enough to get going that "honest" discussion of race that Eric Holder says he wants.

Forgotten White Race Riots and What We Can Learn From Them

In light of the "Fergusons" that have erupted in America over the last 50 years or so, it may come as quite a surprise to many of us to learn that from the 19th century clear through to roughly the middle of the 20th, most of those responsible for initiating "race" riots *were* white.

In 1829, Cincinnati, Ohio had a population of a little more than 2,000 blacks. Within the span of little more than a month, this population would be reduced by half as over 1,000 blacks fled the city as a result of the violence against their person and property initiated by whites—mostly Irish immigrants—who felt economically threatened by the presence of black laborers.

In 1841, another extended outburst of racially-inflamed violence occurred as mobs of whites, in response to a fight that had erupted the previous night between some Irish and black men, took to the streets with clubs in search of blacks to pummel. Black tenants of a boarding house and their neighbors were attacked in their homes.

The violence got worse, though, the next day. According to a witness at the time, when two young whites boys were badly harmed by knife-wielding black assailants, vengeful white men saw to it that blacks were "assaulted wherever" they were "found in the streets," and they were assaulted "with such weapons and violence as to cause death."

In 1863, in Detroit, whites (mostly Irish) spearheaded a rampage against the city's black residents in response to the draft and the detention of a black man who was accused of having raped a white woman. They beat and stoned men and women— including women with small children—and set fire to black businesses and residences.

This same year, the Draft Riots erupted in New York City. To date, this three day conflagration holds the distinction of serving as our country's largest "civil insurrection" of all time. Whites (again, primarily Irish) attacked the Mayor's office, the New York Times building, police officers, fire fighters, white abolitionist women who had married black men and, of course, whatever blacks they could find.

Black businesses, homes, and even a black orphanage were burned to the ground. One black man was fatally battered by hundreds of whites armed with clubs and paving stones. He was hung from a tree and his body set aflame.

However, while he may have been the first, he certainly wasn't the last, for *at least* 100 blacks were murdered from the 13th to the 16th of July during this fateful year. Some estimates place the number as high as 500 black victims claimed by the rioters. Thousands of people were injured.

The military was required to quell the unrest and reclaim control of the city. Many of those blacks who survived the riots fled Manhattan, reducing the black population of the city to its 1820 levels.

Time and space constraints preclude an exhaustive list of white race riots, but suffice it to say that our country's history, up until the middle of the 20th century, is replete with them. Here are just a few:

In 1887, in Louisiana, a mob of whites attacked and killed between 20 to as many as 300 blacks—men, women, and children.

In 1917, in East St. Louis, a group of blacks killed two white police officers after having mistaken them for a carload of white men who had previously shot bullets into a black crowd. In retaliation, white men sought revenge. When it was all over, approximately 100 blacks were dead.

In 1919, in Chicago, a young black male was on a raft on Lake Michigan when he drifted into an area known to be frequented by whites. He was hit by a rock and drowned. When a police officer failed to arrest a suspect, the officer was attacked by blacks.

Whites retaliated, pulling blacks off of trolley cars, pounding them with baseball bats and pieces of iron, and destroying black businesses. Some blacks fought back, but by the time the rioting had ended, more blacks (23) than whites (15) had been killed.

Many, many more incidences of white-on-black (and other white) riots could be cited.

The point of rehashing all of this, however, is not to engage in but another exercise of white guilt mongering. The point is threefold.

First, race riots are not synonymous with black riots. Historically, in America, there have been more white riots than there have been black riots, and in terms of sheer brutality, casualties, and brazenness, the former have made the latter look like temper tantrums.

Second, blacks are not *naturally* more (or less) violent than whites (or anyone else). The appalling amount of black violence that we witness today is a function of a cultural universe of values that is a relatively recent phenomenon, as far as history is measured.

Finally, and perhaps most importantly, this little history lesson is a desperately needed cautionary tale: Just because whites, or at least mobs of whites, are not, in *this day and age,* known for wreaking havoc upon blacks and their communities does *not* mean that such things can't or won't happen in the future.

The past could repeat itself if a tipping point is reached, for just as there is nothing within *the nature* of blacks *as blacks* that accounts for their rioting, so there is nothing within *the nature* of whites *as whites* that explains why they haven't rioted in many decades.

Violence against the persons and property of innocent human beings, no matter their race, is always wrong. But if this isn't enough to deter those who are disposed to commit this evil from doing so, they would be well served to consider that violence just might eventually beget more violence.

When this happens, life becomes unpleasant for everyone.

The Reality of the Trayvon Martin/George Zimmerman Case

George Zimmerman has been acquitted in the shooting death of "the child," the "young boy," Trayvon Martin.

As should go without saying, it is of course a tragedy that our world is such that it regularly claims human life. It is particularly tragic when young people, like Martin, lose their lives in circumstances that could have so easily been avoided.

But Martin was no "child." He was not yet a legal adult, but at 17 years of age he could, with a parent's permission, kill and die for the United States military. And 17 year-olds, particularly when they are six feet tall, intoxicated on drugs, and physically fit, as was Martin, can and do kill and die in the streets of America.

Yet it isn't just Zimmerman's persecutors who are fond of sanitizing Martin's character.

Writing for Front Page Magazine, Arnold Ahlert castigates his fellow conservatives for acting badly.

In "Framing Trayvon," Ahlert contends that "many conservatives" have engaged in a "demonization campaign" against Martin—or "Trayvon," as Ahnert calls him—that runs "parallel" to that promoted against Zimmerman by such "racial arsonists" as Al Sharpton and Jesse Jackson. Conservatives "have hastily embraced caricatures of Trayvon Martin, painting him as a vicious street thug who deserved his fate."

Ahlert insists that Martin sounded like "little more than a rambunctious teenager" whose family and friends describe as "a fine young man," "warm and funny," and "a standout athlete with an enormous appetite."

Where do we begin?

First, Ahlert is correct that, from day one, the "racial arsonists" did indeed rush to demonize Zimmerman. Yet he fails to so much as hint at the fact that the demonization of Zimmerman demanded the *idealization* of Martin. By now, everyone who's paid any attention to this case is all too familiar with the media's tireless juxtaposition of Zimmerman's mug shots alongside the outdated pictures of a prepubescent Martin.

Had Ahlert mentioned this, it would immediately become clear that it isn't "conservatives," but *Martin* who supplied us with a negative caricature of Martin.

More accurately, as details emerged since February of 2012, *time* has exploded the *idyllic caricature* of Martin that the "anti-racists" have labored to embed in the popular imagination.

The Martin who had that fateful encounter with Zimmerman

was a far cry from the 6th grader whose photograph was plastered all over the media for months after the shooting.

As Ahlert himself admits, at the time of his death, Martin "used foul language, made obscene gestures on camera, probably smoked marijuana, and engaged in other troublesome teenage behavior"—like getting caught with possession of what was likely stolen jewelry, getting repeatedly suspended from school, and attempting to assault a bus driver.

This brings us to a second point.

Neither conservatives nor anyone else has made Martin out to be a *vicious* thug, as Ahlert says. What the record shows is that he *was* a thug of a sort, a thug wannabe, if you will. At the very least, he was thug*gish*, even if he may not have been a full blown thug.

And we know this, not just from his record, but solely from the fact that he unleashed a torrent of violence upon Zimmerman.

No one disputes that Martin threw the first punch. From what has been determined, it was he who threw every other punch after that as well. To be clear, there was no *exchange* of blows between Martin and Zimmerman. Rather, Zimmerman was on his back as Martin repeatedly pounded on him.

And it is not as if Zimmerman was in his face posing an imminent danger to Martin. Had this been the case, then perhaps the latter would have been justified in launching a preemptive punch (even if he would not have been justified in punching his face into the ground after he had succeeded in knocking him down).

Had Martin really feared for his life when he noticed that Zimmerman had been following him, and had he conducted himself in a non-thuggish way, then he would have done what Zimmerman did when he first observed Martin: call the authorities. Martin could've ended his phone call with Rachel Jeantel—to whom he referred to Zimmerman as a "creepy ass cracker"—and called the police.

Instead, he chose to lie in wait for Zimmerman before jumping him.

This is the official account of the events of that fateful evening when Martin's life ended—an account that the jury in Florida accepted and that no one has been able to contradict.

Contra Ahlert, to acknowledge these facts is *not* to say that Martin "deserved" to be killed. Much less has anyone, least of all the "conservatives" who Ahlert lectures, even remotely insinuated that Martin deserved to be killed because of his lifestyle.

However, to concede the facts *is* to concede both that Martin did indeed act thuggishly and that Zimmerman was just as justified in shooting him as an elderly woman would be justified in shooting an assailant who had her pinned on the ground while striking her.

Though painful, we mustn't lose sight of the realities of this issue—even if the Zimmerman haters, including some alleged "conservatives," insist upon calling them "caricatures."

Some Questions for Eric Holder

While being interviewed recently by ABC News' Pierre Thomas, Attorney General Eric Holder expressed his belief that he and Barack Obama have been subjected to a measure of "vehemence" unlike that with which other public figures have had to reckon.

Anyone who's been alive for more than a few years doesn't need this spelled out for them, but Holder couldn't resist the impulse to make explicit the point at which he's always driving: For Obama's and Holder's critics who are always "talking about taking their country back," there is "a certain racial component," "a racial animus," that animates them.

To put it more bluntly, Holder is accusing his opponents of being a bunch of "*racists.*"

Of course, no one should be in the least bit surprised by this. Holder, like his boss, has always been a "Johnny One-Note" when it comes to the issue of race. But rather than go on the defensive, as whites generally and white conservatives always do, let us instead pose some questions to the AG.

First, by "racial animus" you presumably mean "racism." But what does *this* mean, Mr. Holder?

In spite of—or maybe because of—the ease with this term is hurled about, "racism" has come to mean all things to all people: Adolph Hitler, Nazis, Klansmen, Republicans, conservatives, libertarians, John Wayne, Southerners, Germans, American police officers and military personnel, slave masters and abolitionists, the Union and the Confederacy, America's Founders, elderly whites, middle class whites, our judicial system, our political arrangements, academia, Hollywood, "the media," and so forth and so on, have all been accused of "racism."

However, as we say, if everyone is "racist," then no one is "racist." Or, if you will, if "racism" means anything and everything, then it means nothing.

Yet maybe, Mr. Holder, by "racist" you have in mind simply someone who dislikes black people, like yourself and the President, simply and solely because they are black. Given the context of your comments, I suspect that this is probably your meaning.

The unanimously acknowledged "father" of modern philosophy, Rene Descartes, identified as an axiom of reason the proposition that "something can't come from nothing." And since, sir, you and those of your ilk are forever looking for "root causes" whenever it comes to accounting for the dysfunctional conduct of which America's "ghettoes" are ridden, I am inclined to think that you too believe it is self-evident that from nothing, nothing comes.

So, *if*, as you're so certain, your critics dislike you and Mr. Obama only because you both are black, answer me this: from whence springs this sentiment of theirs? Why would anyone, white or otherwise, dislike black people? In other words, what are the "root causes" of white "racism?"

Bear in mind, sir, that the stock replies—"That's just how white 'racists' were raised;" "Whites entertain 'racist' stereotypes about blacks," etc.—are alike viciously question-begging (to say nothing of sounding "stereotypical" themselves). Each in its own way simply rephrases the claim that whites are "racist."

And if you resolve, Mr. Attorney General, to concede that some of these negative "stereotypes" about blacks do indeed have a basis in reality but are nevertheless a "legacy" of white "racism," please note that, once more, you beg the question by restating your original assertion: whites are/were "racist."

It's okay, though, if you can't answer this query Mr. Holder. If I was a betting man I'd bet my house that never, ever have you had to give it any thought at all.

Of real logical axioms like that identified by Descartes' I'm sure you couldn't care less. What you *do* care about, however, and care about more than anything else, is the proposition that whites are "racists" and blacks are unqualified victims. *This* you treat as a first principle of reason.

And this brings me to my next question: it's true, isn't it Mr. Holder, that you *like* crying "racism" precisely *because* blacks are widely portrayed (by people like yourself) as victims?

Contrary to what many of your critics claim, I for one most definitely do *not* believe that you charge them with "racism" simply and solely for the purpose of immunizing yourself and the President against criticism (though this certainly is *a* consideration some of the time). I believe that you work long and hard at convincing *yourself* that the two of you—the two most powerful human beings on the planet, mind you—really *are* victims of "racism."

To put it another way, your charges of "racism" are not just politically motivated, are they? Ideologically and even psychologically, you and Mr. Obama—children of "privilege," the two of you—*need* to believe that you are both "authentically black"—i.e. "oppressed"—and "down with the struggle"—i.e. "oppressed."

Your interests are served well by the perception that you and Mr. Obama are unpopular because of your skin pigmentation, aren't they Mr. Holder?

The problem, however, is that this lie in which you and Obama have invested your whole being is a great *disservice* to the interests of the rest of us—regardless of our skin color.

Obliging Eric Holder: Toward that Honest Discussion of Race

It isn't just orgies of violence and destruction that the acquittal of George Zimmerman has provoked. This verdict also renewed Attorney General Eric Holder's call for an "honest" discussion of race, a discussion that, he maintains, Americans continue to defer.

I am second to none in my contempt for Holder, but, in this case, he couldn't be more correct:

Americans have *not* discussed race *honestly*. Nor will they do so as long as, ironically, *the Eric Holders* of the world continue to have their way.

For all his cries for a truthful dialogue on race, Holder, like the man to whom he answers and their fellow ideologues in the Racism-Industrial-Complex, is deeply invested in fortifying the pack of bald-faced lies that are American racial politics. So, with an eye toward dismantling these lies and heeding Holder's request for straight talk, I submit the following questions to get the conversation going.

Traditionally, Americans have endorsed what has been called "the one drop" rule. According to this rule, if a person has any (black) African ancestry whatsoever, he or she is black. Well, since George Zimmerman's great-grandfather was black, doesn't this mean that *he* is black? After all, had Zimmerman lived in the antebellum South, the knowledge that he had "black blood" in his veins alone would have sufficed to make him as eligible a candidate for slavery as Trayvon Martin would have been.

In turn, doesn't this mean that the Zimmerman/Martin case is but another *black-on-black* shooting?

If so, why, of the astronomical number of instances of black-on-black violence that occur in America on a regular basis and that Holder and his ilk ignore, are they determined to make, quite literally, a *federal* case out of this one instance of such violence? If not, if, unlike Barack Obama and Holder himself, Zimmerman somehow defies the one-drop rule, how or why does this justify treating the shooting death of Trayvon Martin far differently than the shooting deaths of the thousands of blacks who are shot dead annually by other blacks?

It is a twisted subculture of the black underclass that underwrites the epidemic of black violence. Far from being condemned, it has been romanticized and/or excused (by people like Holder and Obama). However, countless numbers of young black males like Martin imbibe a warped sense of masculinity from this ghetto ethos of which gangsta' rap and hip hop are the most popular vehicles. May not this have had at least some role to play in Martin's fate—as well as that of the legions of young blacks that kill and are killed on a daily basis in this country?

In an honest discussion of race, isn't it imperative that we finally express at least a fraction of the outrage over the shocking rates of black-on-*white* violence that was expressed by Holder and the like over the killing of Trayvon Martin? It goes without saying that if whites were targeting blacks to the extent to which blacks target whites, no one—least of all Holder—would stand for it.

So why do such "anti-racists" as Holder and Obama endorse this grotesque double standard, standards that sanction the debasement of white life while confirming the suspicions of an ever growing number of whites that "anti-racism" is really just code for anti-*white*?

Why is black criminality and violence invariably explained

away by "anti-racists" in terms of "root causes," but when racial animus is directed, or is even, as in the case of George Zimmerman, *alleged* to have been directed *against* blacks, there is no search for any "root causes?" In the case of Zimmerman, say, his property and that of those in his lower-middle class community had been besieged by people who fit a certain profile—a profile that Trayvon Martin matched. Is it not fair to think that had Zimmerman and his neighbors not suffered these injustices, that maybe he wouldn't have been quite as suspicious of Martin that fateful night?

We use the words "racial unrest" and "race riots" in characterizing exhibitions of mayhem of the kind that are unfolding the wake of the Zimmerman verdict. Why? Such terms suggest *a clash* between the race*s*. In reality, from at least the beginning of the second half of the last century to the present, so-called "*race*" riots have actually been *black* riots.

When Klansmen used to spread terror throughout black communities, no one referred to these episodes as "race riots." Neither do we do so today when recalling those times. So, again, why, do we use this term to describe mobs of blacks who target whites?

There are plenty more topics that would be addressed in a genuinely honest discussion of race.

These are just some questions that come immediately to mind in the aftermath of the Zimmerman verdict.

I won't hold my breath waiting for those who claim to want an honest discussion of race to respond honestly to them—or respond to them at all.

Zora Neale Hurston: Another Politically Inconvenient Black American

February is Black History Month. As those on the right (and even an increasing number of people elsewhere) know well enough, these four weeks are all too easily used by activists as an opportunity to promote a politics of victimhood congenial to a leftist agenda.

The famed black writer—*and conservative*—Zora Neale Hurston, frustrates this program.

Born in the early 1890's in the lower South, Hurston would one day join the ranks of those black writers who became associated with "the Harlem Renaissance." Unlike most of her colleagues, however, she staunchly rejected the communism and socialism with which they sympathized.

Hurston resented the efforts made by black and white intellectual alike to make of black Americans a new proletariat, a victim class perpetually in need of an all-encompassing national government to ease the "lowdown dirty deal" that "nature has somehow given them [.]"

Hurston was adamant that she was "not tragically colored." She insisted that "no great sorrow" lies "damned up in my soul, lurking behind my eyes," and she placed a world of distance between herself and "the sobbing school of negrohood who hold that nature somehow has given them a lowdown dirty deal and whose feelings are hurt about it [.]"

For what contemporary black commentator Larry Elder refers to as the "victicrats" among us, Hurston had zero use. "Someone is always at my elbow reminding me that I am the granddaughter of slaves," she remarked. Much to their chagrin, though, "it fails to register depression with me." Furthermore, she stated bluntly that "slavery is the price I paid for civilization."

Our increasingly joyless generation is oblivious to another of Hurston's insights: a sense of humor can bear most, if not all, painful things. Regarding racial discrimination, she noted that while she "sometimes" feels "discriminated against," she does not get "angry" about it. Rather, the experience "merely astonishes me," for how, Hurston asks, "can any deny themselves the pleasure of my company? It's beyond me."

As far as foreign policy was concerned, Hurston was of the *old* right. She was what today we are inclined to call a "*paleo*conservative" or "*paleo*libertarian." With the Russell Kirks, Patrick J. Buchanans, and Ron Pauls of the right Hurston had much in common—especially when it came to foreign policy.

Of the Roosevelt and Truman administrations, she spoke contemptuously as she identified what Hurston took as their hypocrisy. Those "people who claim that it is a noble thing to die for freedom and democracy," she asserted, "wax frothy if anyone points out the inconsistency of their morals [.]" The fact is that "we" also "consider machine gun bullets good laxatives for heathens who get constipated with toxic ideas about a country of their own." Roosevelt "can call names across an ocean" for his "four freedoms," she added, yet he lacked "the courage to speak even softly at home."

When Truman dropped "the bomb" on Japan, Hurston referred to him as "the Butcher of Asia."

But Hurston blasted away at Big Government for domestic purposes as well. She was an adamant critic of the New Deal and jumped at the chance to support presidential candidate Robert A. Taft when the opportunity arose for Republicans to dismantle the house that Roosevelt built.

A big part of FDR's legacy, Hurston complained, is that "the word 'liberal' is now an unstable and devious thing in connotation [.]" What this means in practice is "Pinkos and other degrees of fellow travelers" have succeeded in convincing large numbers of people that a liberal "is a person who desires greater Government control and Federal handouts."

Taft, though, could put an end to this, Hurston claimed, for Taft is a *real* liberal, a *Jeffersonian* liberal.

Interestingly, Hurston found Taft's lack of charisma to be among his virtues, for she realized that those presidents who seduced the electorate with their charms were dangerous to liberty. Taft, she thought, was more like "those men who held high office" before "the mob took over" with "the advent of Jacksonian democracy [.]"

An opponent of segregation, Hurston was just as much of an opponent of federal efforts—like *Brown v. Board of Education*—to end it. She was bewildered by the idea that, as a black person, she should take comfort in the fact that there was now "a court order for somebody to associate with me who does not wish me near them [.]"

Race relations in the South, through the "effort and time" of *those who live there,* "will work out all its problems."

In short, Hurston was a devotee of *liberty.* She relished in her individuality while courageously discarding the collectivist, utopian fantasies of which the twentieth century was ridden:

> *I have the nerve to walk my own way, however hard, in my search for reality, rather than climb upon the rattling wagon of wishful illusions.*

During this Black History Month, all lovers of liberty would be well served to follow Hurston's lead.

Institutional Racism: If you are White, You are Racist

The view that "racism" is limited to the prejudices of individuals and/or the discriminatory policies of the government dies hard.

Those who have thought longest and hardest on the evil of racism—the "experts"—have been telling us for quite some time that racism contaminates the very *institutions* or "structures" of Western civilization. The philosopher Richard Wasserstrom is a case in point. While "institutional racism" is more "subtle" and "unintentional" than more covert or traditional expressions of racism, it is also the most intractable for this reason.

In fact, institutional racism pervades our very *concepts.* "Quite often," Wasserstrom explains, "without realizing it," our concepts "take for granted certain objectionable aspects of racist ideology without our being aware of it."

Take for example the concept of "a common humanity," a concept that supplies the philosophical backbone of such related concepts as the rule of law, equality before the law, the dignity of persons, and the ideal of "color blindness." Though treated by most people as an *antidote* to racism, the concept of a common humanity *reinforces* racism.

Moreover, it makes it that much more difficult to defeat the latter.

As the political scientist Iris Marion Young informs us, in spite of posing as "neutral and universal," the concept of a common humanity is a "culturally and experientially specific" instrument by which whites, and white men particularly, "structure privilege and oppression." That is, "cultural imperialism" continues courtesy of the ideal of a common humanity. Young writes: "Blindness to difference [color-blindness] perpetuates cultural imperialism by allowing norms expressing the point of view and experience of privileged groups [whites] to appear neutral and universal."

The verdict is inescapable: white people are incorrigibly racist. How can matters be otherwise when the very ideas that whites use to *combat* racism are themselves racist?

If racism really is embodied in our institutions, our modes of perceiving our world, then it is as ubiquitous as is the air we breathe. It is omnipresent. And if it is omnipresent, then there is no place to which we can turn to evade it.

Whites are incorrigibly racist.

The great philosopher David Hume observed that the more general and abstract an idea is, the more plausible it is. When we spell it out in the concrete the idea of institutional racism, there is no getting around the following.

If you are a white, you are a racist. So too are your children racist.

Since I am white, I am a racist, as is my three year-old son.

The 20 children gunned down in Newtown, Connecticut, are racist.

Gabbie Giffords is a racist.

The four Americans murdered during the latest attack on an American embassy in Libya are racist.

Abraham Lincoln, Joe Biden, FDR, Glenn Armstrong, Frank Sinatra, George Washington, Dick Clark, Andy Griffith, Bill and Hillary Clinton, Bill Maher, Sean Penn, Audie Murphy, and the mostly white firefighters who rushed into the World Trade Center towers on 9/11 to rescue strangers are all racist.

Chris Mathews, Ed Shultz, St. Francis of Assisi, Quentin Tarantino, Michael Moore, and Rachel Maddow are racist.

The most saintly of whites no less than the most evil, the most committed anti-racists no less than the most virulent neo-Nazi skinheads and Klan members, are alike racist.

Richard Wasserstrom and Iris Marion Young, both white, are racist.

Those white editors who will refuse to publish this article for fear of being portrayed as racist are as racist as those who have no such fears.

There are still other implications of the claim that racism is "institutional."

If even the most seemingly innocuous, anti-racist of the concepts in which whites routinely trade are mired in racism, then *the concept that racism is immoral* is also racist! The thought that everyone deserves to be treated equally regardless of their race is a racist thought, for it is a thought that was conspicuously absent from the Earth until men of European decent fought hard for it.

Translation: in advocating on behalf of measures that benefit, or ostensibly benefit, racial minorities—the abolition of slavery and Jim Crow, say, and "affirmative action"—non-whites prove just how "culturally imperialistic"—how racist—they remain.

If institutional racism is a reality, then every single white person is a racist. And if we want to overcome racism, then the only way to do so is by "fundamentally transforming"—i.e. repealing and replacing—Western civilization.

Ideologically Inconvenient Slavery: Islamic Masters, Infidel Slaves

Agents of the Racism-Industrial-Complex (RIC) are forever wailing from the rooftops over the fact that whites once enslaved blacks in America.

But there are some crucial facts that they omit from the narrative of White Oppression and Black Victimhood.

First, from the mists of time until the 18th century, slavery had been a universal institution, endorsed by religious and non-religious moralists alike. The very word "slave" stems from "*Slav,*" which in turn derives from the Slavish people's experience of having been enslaved en masse by North African Muslims.

There is scarcely a person alive today whose ancestors weren't *both* enslavers and enslaved. Yet it wasn't until the late 1700's that, for the first time, a moral backlash erupted against this age-old institution, a revolt *in England* spearheaded by people who—horror of horrors!—were *white, Christian business men.* Such was their vigilance that they soon swayed the British Empire, which in turn brought the full weight of their military and economic weight to bear upon Africans, Arabs, and Asians who had to be coerced into abandoning the practice of slave-trading.

Other European countries, and their offshoots, like America, soon enough followed suit. Thanks to their efforts—the tireless endeavors of just those people upon whose shoulders "anti-racist" ideologues lay *sole* blame for slavery (and every other scourge)—slavery is now illegal everywhere. That RIC agents act as if none of this history happened proves just how invested they are in peddling their ideological fictions.

Their neglect of politically-inconvenient circumstances in *the present* is also telling.

While slavery is illegal, it is nevertheless still practiced in a variety of places. By some estimates, there are more slaves today than there has been at any time in the past.

And nowhere is slavery more common, and more brutal, than in the Islamic world.

The Daily Mail relays some of the unspeakable cruelty to which Yazidi women *and girls* have been subjected by their Islamic State captors.

A 19 year-old female from the Yazidi community in Iraq revealed the extent of her courage in sharing with the world details of her time spent as a slave to ISIS.

Hamshe was married and pregnant when ISIS jihadists stormed her community, murdered the men—including, she is nearly sure, her husband—and made slaves of her and the other females. Hamshe relays that one of the militants threatened to lock her in a room and withhold all food and water unless she agreed to *marry* him.

While in the custody of her captors, Hamshe gave birth. After 28 days as a slave, she managed to escape with her child. Thankfully, after a harrowing trek, she was reunited with her family.

But her life is forever different, and Hamshe confesses that the memory of jihadists wrenching women and children from their men and carting them off as "war spoils" will forever be seared into her consciousness. Her mother, though eternally grateful for the return of her daughter, says bluntly that both their family and the Yazidi community have been "*destroyed.*"

Most of these women are not as fortunate as Hamshe.

And many aren't *women* but *girls* as young as 12 years of age who are repeatedly, violently raped, beaten, and sold into slavery and marriage.

But that's not all.

These female slaves of ISIS are subjected to *blood transfusions* for the purpose of supplying blood for wounded ISIS fighters.

A 21 year-old Yazidi woman who claimed to have refused to be "gift" to the head of ISIS—Abu Bakir Al Baghdadi—spoke at length about the horrors that she witnessed.

> *I saw everything, I saw girls being raped. I witnessed their torture. I saw babies separated from their mothers. Some children were 5 or 6 years old when they were taken from their families.*

The survivor said that there was "no horror" that she hadn't experienced. She witnessed the murders of "our fathers, uncles, and everyone." She also tells of a 13 year-old girl who was locked in the home of an ISIS head who raped her for three days—even though he told *his children* that he was instructing her in the Koran.

Two sisters tried to strangle one another after being abducted by ISIS and awaiting their sale to men who promised to make them their wives. They would've succeeded had it not been for their fellow captives who separated them. Other women also attempt suicide, but are deterred by ISIS militants who promise to murder their families in the event that they kill themselves.

One escaped slave described how ISIS militants would drag young girls by their hair to be carried off into a living nightmare. Another said that some "girls" who had been brutalized while enslaved would be returned until they healed—and then *resold*. All of the *girls* were sold *before* the women. No amount of crying and pleading moved the Islamic State barbarians.

ISIS published a document regarding some rules for slavery. While announcing their belief that Christians, Jews, and Yazidis can become slaves to Muslim masters, they followed this up with the following:

> **Question:** *Is it allowed to have intercourse with a female captive immediately after taking possession of her?*
> **Answer:** *If she is a virgin, her master can have intercourse with her immediately after taking possession. But if she is not, you must make sure that she is not pregnant.*
> **Question:** *Is it allowed to have intercourse with a female slave who has not reached puberty?*
> **Answer:** *You may have intercourse with a female slave who hasn't reached puberty if she is fit for intercourse. However, if she is not fit for intercourse, it is enough to enjoy her without.*

These monsters are thriving now. But rather than address any of this, RIC agents in Washington, the media, and academia would prefer to talk about white slave masters and traders from more than 150 years ago.

The Realities of Inter-racial Crime in America

In almost every instance of the so-called "knock out game," perpetrators have been black and their victims mostly white (and/or) Asian. There is *one*—and *only* one—case in which the racial dynamics of this violence reversed course, an incident from Texas involving a white predator and a black prey.

Not unsurprisingly, this is the only instance of "the game" that Barack Obama's Department of Justice is choosing to pursue as a "hate crime."

And it is the one and only incident regarding which Katie Couric unreservedly disclosed the respective races of the perpetrator and victim on her daily television show. As for the phenomenon generally, Couric was careful to convey the impression that it was racially-neutral, an activity in which "kids" of all races routinely engaged.

Couric's take was all too predictable.

It is also a lie, a lie of omission, for like that of all of her colleagues in the left-leaning media, it is painfully clear that Couric's objective is to manipulate the public into thinking that this phenomenon is something that it isn't.

In reality, though, Couric is simply doing with this racial issue what leftists have been doing with the issue of race for a long, long time.

Consider slavery, *the* lynchpin of the narrative underwriting racial politics in America.

To know only the conventional account of slavery is to know worse than nothing. It is to know *next to* nothing—just enough truth, however miniscule, to make one think that one knows the whole truth.

According to the conventional narrative, whites originally kidnapped blacks from some idyllic African paradise for the sake of reducing them to a lifetime of servitude in America.

In other words, only white Americans were slave masters and only blacks were slaves.

In reality, slavery is an institution that is as old, and as universal, as humanity itself. People of all races have both enslaved and been enslaved. Tellingly, the word "slave" derives from the experience of the *Slavish,* an Eastern European—i.e. white—ethnic group whose members were enslaved *en masse* by North African Muslims for a period of nearly two centuries.

Those poor souls who were made to endure the unfathomable evils of the notorious "Middle Passage" were *sold* by other black Africans, slave traders who were doing nothing other than engaging in one of Africa's oldest, and most lucrative, practices. To this day, long after Europeans employed their economic and military might to *force*, not just Africans, but other "people of color" in Asia and the Middle East, to abolish this abominable industry, slavery continues in parts of "the Dark continent."

The reader may also be unaware of the fact that in early America, the sight of *white* slaves—not indentured *servants*, but *slaves*—was not an uncommon one at the slave ports. And in the antebellum South, as late as 1860, there were as many as *three thousand* black slave *masters*.

Another inconvenient tidbit that the ideologically approved tale of slavery omits is that, long before whites discovered the New World, slavery had been ubiquitous among the indigenous peoples of what would become the Americas.

So, while whites most certainly did participate in slavery, to know only this is to know next to nothing, for it suggests that there is something uniquely wicked about whites. But if there is anything at all unique about whites with respect to this issue it is that whites—and white English Christians to boot!—were the first (and only) people in all of human history to spearhead a moral revolt against this perennial trade in human bondage.

As Thomas Sowell and others have long documented, during the apex of the British Empire, the English deployed their immense power, against considerable resistance on the part of Africans and others, to stamp out slavery throughout the world.

Just the slightest acquaintance with real history brings into focus a dramatically different picture of slavery than that advanced by the politically useful racial fiction of opportunists and activists.

Similarly, a dramatically distorted picture of "the knock out game" emerges after Katie Couric and company have left the reality on their editing room floors.

Evil in Knoxville

To judge from the ghastly details of "The Wichita Massacre" that I described earlier, it is difficult not to think that this abomination of a crime supplies us with as blatant an expression of unmitigated evil as any that we're likely to encounter.

Indeed, Reginald Carr and his brother Jonathan *are* in fact the "soulless monsters" that one of their two surviving victims described them as being, and if they were white and their victims were black—rather than the other way around—there isn't a person in America who wouldn't have long known this.

Yet as a reader was quick to note, there is another crime that occurred in Knoxville, Tennessee in 2007 that rivals, and may, if this is possible, even *exceed* the massacre in Wichita for its raw savagery.

Like the case in Wichita, "the Knoxville Horror," as it's dubbed by those relatively few interested souls that dared to report on it, has received virtually no national coverage.

And like the case in Wichita, the perpetrators in Knoxville were black and their prey white.

By all accounts, Channon Christian, a 21 year-old senior at the University of Tennessee who lived at home with her parents and brother, was as beautiful on the inside as she was on the outside. Her boyfriend, a 23 year-old trim carpenter named Christopher Newsom, was equally beloved by lots of friends and family.

Little could either one of them have known that when they left their parents' homes on the night of January 7, 2007, they would never see their loved ones again.

On this fateful Saturday evening, Channon and "Chris" had planned upon going to a friend's birthday party. Chris arrived to meet Channon at another friend's apartment so that he could follow her to the party in his own car. But first he escorted Channon to her own car where he leaned over to give her a kiss.

And that's where the young couple was greeted by thugs who carjacked and abducted them at gunpoint.

Channon and Chris were driven to the rundown residence of their assailants: George "Detroit" Thomas; Letalvis "Rome" Cobbins; Lemaricus "Slim" Davidson; Eric "E" Boyd; and Vanessa Coleman. It at this house of horrors that Channon and Chris would be subjected to a species of brutality that defies the imagination—and that would, ultimately, culminate in their deaths.

According to the *Knoxville News Sentinel*, a medical examiner—Dr. Darinka Mileusnic-Polchan—testified at the trial of one of the defendants that "[Chris] Newsom was repeatedly raped and then blindfolded, gagged, arms and feet bound and his head covered." Then, while "barefoot, he was either led or dragged outside the house to a set of nearby railroad tracks, where a gun was placed to the back of his head and fired.

He was shot twice more, once in the neck and once in the back."

Finally, his "body was...set on fire [.]"

His body was set on fire.

Channon, though, wouldn't die until hours later—after unrelenting "sexual torture."

The *Knoxville News Sentinel* reports: "[Channon] Christian suffered horrific injuries to her vagina, anus, and mouth. She was not only raped, but savaged with 'an object'...She was beaten in the head. Some type of chemical was poured down her throat, and her body, including her bleeding and battered genital area, likely scrubbed by the same solution [.]"

As if the specifics of her ordeal weren't dreadful enough, the paper informs readers that it occurred "*all while Christian was alive*" (emphasis added) [.]

Yet Channon's nightmare was not over.

"She was then 'hog-tied,' with curtains and strips of bedding, her face covered tightly with a small white trash bag and her body stashed inside five large trash bags before being placed inside a large trash can and covered with sheets."

The medical examiner concluded that "Christian died slowly, suffocating [.]"

The parents of Channon Christian and Chris Newsom have been made to endure not only the trauma of losing their children, and losing them to a gang of conscienceless demons. Not unlike the families of the Carrs' victims in Wichita, they've also had to suffer the indignity of witnessing *new* trials ordered—and on the flimsiest of grounds—for their children's rapist-murderers: the judge who presided over the first set of trials, it was argued, had a drug problem during the last couple of years of his tenure that rendered him incompetent.

This pathetic argument worked—much to the chagrin of the jurors who made it clear in no uncertain terms that it was *they* who convicted the villains, and that they were quite competent when they did so.

Thankfully, however, verdicts delivered the second time around weren't all that different in substance from those originally issued (though the sheer fact that any of these gutter snipes continue to avail themselves of oxygen is itself an injustice):

The ringleader, Lemaricus "Slim" Davidson remains on death row; Letalvis "Rome" Cobbins is serving a life sentence without parole, while George "Detroit" Thomas serves a sentence of 123 years to life; Eric "E" Boyd, who was convicted of his role in the carjacking—a federal offense—and for his assistance in helping the others evade capture, is doing 18 years in a federal penitentiary; and Vanessa Coleman is serving a 35 year sentence—but she will be eligible for parole in early 2019.

Most of us are familiar with the old saying, "Charity begins at home." So too, then, must the fight against evil—the fight in which those in Republican-friendly media outlets are constantly imploring us to engage when discussing *the rest of the world*—begin at home. As the Wichita and Knoxville atrocities make painfully clear, evil does not end at America's borders.

But the first step toward fighting evil is calling it for what it is—even when its agents (and their victims) make it "politically incorrect" to do so.

Inter-racial Attacks the "Anti-Racist" Media Ignored

For weeks on end, the police shooting death of a black man in Ferguson, Missouri by a white officer had managed to remain front and center on the national stage. The usual suspects in the Racism-Industrial-Complex (RIC) held up this incident as proof that "black men in America are *under attack,*" or some gibberish along these lines.

The truth, of course, is dramatically otherwise, a fact of which no remotely aware or honest human being needs any reminding.

For starters, black men in America *are* under attack. But the predators responsible are not whites, whether police officers are otherwise; rather, *they are other black men.*

Yet, if "racism" is the mother of all evils, a "cancer" to society, as we have been tirelessly told for decades and decades, then the exorbitant rate of black-*on-black* violence, while dreadful as far as it goes, should nevertheless register lower on our scale of priorities than the comparably obscene level of black-*on-white* violence—which, scandalously, doesn't seem to register at all.

After all, if the roles were reversed and whites were attacking blacks to a fraction of the extent to which blacks currently attack whites, there is no one—and least of all no one among the captains of RIC—who would hesitate to cite this as *proof* that "racism" was alive and well.

Just this past week, four vicious black-on-white attacks made local news in their respective towns—while, all too predictably, being entirely neglected by the national media.

In Lockport, New York, two black teenage *girls* were captured on video savagely pummeling a white girl upon luring her to the location of their choice. According to News 4, WIVB, a 12 year-old and a 15 year-old "befriended" their "victim and tricked her" into convening with them in an "alleyway" known by the residents of Lockport as "Works Place."

That's when the beating commenced.

Reports News 4: "The video shows the victim being pulled to the ground by her hair and being repeatedly punched and kicked in the face."

The victim was repeatedly punched and kicked in the face.

But it gets worse.

One of the brutes "repeatedly stomps on her [the victim's] head."

And all of this happens *before* the older of the two attackers punches the victim some more.

In Memphis, Tennessee, a large group of black teenagers—according to witnesses, 100-125 of them—forced the owner of a pizza restaurant to close an hour earlier than usual before it stormed a 25 year-old white customer at nearby Kroger's. The victim was beaten to a bloody pulp.

While he lay unconscious, his assailants took turns kicking and punching him. They even slammed a pumpkin on his head—all while he was cold-cocked. A witness relayed that "all [that] you could see was blood and pumpkins."

A black female who was videoing the event can be heard laughing away as she screeches, "they got a white dude!"

Two employees—at least one of whom, reportedly, was black—were also pounded into oblivion when they tried to intervene to spare the first victim from the further ravages of the wolf pack.

In a suburb of Kansas City, just a few days ago, *five* elderly white people—two men and three women—were murdered by a 34 year-old black man, ex-convict Brandon Howell. George and Ann Taylor, both of whom were in their late 80's, were *beaten* to death in their own home.

Howell then fatally gunned down 88 year-old Lorene Hurst, her 63 year-old son Darrel, and 69 year-old Susan Choucroun.

To top it all off, Howell then sped away in the Taylors' car.

In New York City, two black women forced their way into the apartment of three white residents in an attempt to force them *out* of their apartment and out of their Brooklyn neighborhood.

The aggressors also robbed their victims at gunpoint while complaining that they were "tired [of] white people moving into the area."

Each of these incidents occurred within just the last week or so, in towns in disparate regions of the country.

And yet we hear not a peep about any of it from the national media.

It isn't, however, just the left-wing (misnamed) "mainstream" media that is silent on this score.

Equally silent are "mainstream" "conservatives" in the so-called "alternative" media. Fox certainly hasn't broached this topic. Nor has "conservative" radio done so.

This bi-partisan silence is telling. Had whites been the predators in the foregoing cases and blacks the prey, the left would be apoplectic, and the usual suspects would be moaning and groaning over the need for an "honest" discussion of race and "racism." Had the culprits been Arabic Muslims, you could bet the bank that "conservative" media would be all abuzz over it.

But the reality is that in contemporary America, it isn't whites or Arabic Muslims who are the biggest purveyors of interracial violence; it is blacks who hold this ugly distinction.

And this is something that all those who renounce evil must have the courage to confront.

The Politically Inconvenient Malcolm X

This year isn't just the golden anniversary of Selma. It is as well marks the 50th anniversary of the murder of Malcolm X.

Malcolm X has been mythologized. According to the myth, there are, essentially, *two* Malcolms: the "pre-Mecca" Malcolm and the "post-Mecca" Malcolm X. The former, a national minister for Elijah Muhammad's Nation of Islam, preached black separatism. The latter, in glaring contrast, rejected the Nation and promoted interracial unity.

That this is revisionism at its best (or worst) is gotten easily enough from the inconvenient facts that it omits:

(1) Malcolm X taught that *the white race* was *the creation* of an evil black scientist named Yacub.

(2) Malcolm as well taught that history would culminate in a racial Armageddon in which God would enable blacks to bring about the extermination of the white race. And how would this occur? According to Malcolm X biographer Bruce Perry, Malcolm, following Elijah Muhammad, informed his congregants of "the mother ship," a "wheel-shaped flying saucer that contained hundreds of 'baby planes.' Each baby plane carried bombs filled with two tons of a powerful explosive. Piloting the planes, he said, were men who had been trained to fly since the age of six—men who had never smiled."

(3) In 1962 a French airliner crashed and 121 whites from Georgia were killed. Malcolm's response seems not to have made it into any of the collections of his quotations: "I should like to announce a very beautiful thing that has happened. I got a wire from God today. He really answered our prayers over in France…We will continue to pray, and we hope that every day another plane falls out of the sky."

(4) Whites, Malcolm taught, were "devils." But it

157

wasn't just whites for whom he reserved his venom. His black rivals he showered with degrading insults as well. Take, for example, Malcolm's public comments on Martin Luther King, Jr.

King, Malcolm said, was "a chump, not a champ." King was "a little black mouse sitting on top of a big white elephant" [the United States]. When King received the Nobel Peace Prize, Malcolm publicly remarked: "He got the Peace Prize; we got the problem." Malcolm added: "I don't want the white man giving me medals." King, he said, "is the best thing that ever happened to white folks. *For* white folks! As long as anybody can keep Negroes nonviolent, it helps white folks."

By the way, Malcolm X made these remarks *after* his split with the Nation of Islam.

(5) On January 28, 1961, Malcolm met with the Ku Klux Klan in Atlanta, Georgia. On behalf of the Nation of Islam, he sought to elicit help from the Klan in obtaining land in the South that could be used as an independent nation for black Americans. According to Bruce Perry, Malcolm blamed Jews for hijacking the civil rights movement by promoting integration, and he expressed his dismay to the Klansmen that they hadn't yet killed King.

(6) Booker T. Washington, Malcolm said, was a "white man's nigger," Jackie Robinson and Joe Louis were "stooges" for "the white man," and the NAACP was a "black body with a white head." In fact, as far as Malcolm was concerned, every black integrationist was either a "Quisling" or an "Uncle Tom."

Malcolm X did *not* split with the Nation of Islam; the Nation split with Malcolm.

Against Elijah Muhammad's orders to refrain from commenting on the assassination of JKF, Malcolm remarked to the media that Kennedy's murder was a case of "the chickens coming home to roost" and that this made him "glad." Livid, Muhammad reacted, and Malcolm was in effect shown the door.

But this wasn't the end of it: Malcolm threw himself at "the Messenger's" mercy by beseeching him, on multiple occasions, to reinstate him—all to no avail.

It was *then* that Malcolm retaliated by publically charging his former mentor with having fathered at least eight illegitimate children with several of Muhammad's young assistants.

And it was then that the call for Malcolm's head was issued.

In desperate need of a new public relations image, Malcolm made his trek to Mecca where, after a mere eleven days, he returned to the states a new man, a champion of the brotherhood of all men.

Sure.

Malcolm founded a new organization, the Organization for African American Unity (OAAU). Its newspaper continued to feature the same incendiary racial rhetoric—e.g. headlines like "Racist America"—for which Malcolm was known, and Malcolm himself pledged to haul the United States government before the United Nations for its violation of the "human rights" of its black citizens.

However, on February 21, 1965, while about to address a crowd at the Audubon Ballroom in Harlem, thugs from the organization to which Malcolm committed his adult life—thugs whose frame of mind he did as much as anyone to shape—filled him with bullets. Such was the determination of his fellow black Muslims—*not* the United States government—to avenge "the Honorable" Elijah Muhammad that even the knowledge that Malcolm's pregnant wife and four little daughters were in attendance didn't suffice to deter them.

These are just some of the ugly details that don't make the cut when it comes to the mythology surrounding Malcolm X.

Nelson Mandela: The Untold Story

Given that the entire planet seems to be of one voice in both mourning the loss of Nelson Mandela and celebrating his life, most will find it inconceivable that anyone would think to so much as suggest that Mandela was anything less than the saint that his admirers are working tirelessly to depict him as.

But truth is truth and Mandela was no saint.

Mandela was a proponent of "democratic socialism" who, along with the South African Communist Party, unleashed a torrent of violence against his political opponents that included the bombing of government sites. He was convicted of "sabotage" and attempting to overthrow the government—charges to which he openly confessed at his trial.

And in spite of having been released from prison in 1990 after serving 27 years and eventually becoming South Africa's first black president, he remained on the United States Terror Watch list until as recently as 2008.

The late Margaret Thatcher characterized Mandela's African National Congress as a "typical terrorist organization."

Ilana Mercer is a writer and former resident of South Africa who knows all too well about Mandela and his legacy. One of her books, *Into the Cannibal's Pot: Lessons for America from Post-Apartheid South Africa,* includes a chapter chock full of interesting, but inconvenient, facts regarding the man who is now being lauded as never before.

Mercer informs us that long before apartheid came crumbling down, the government of South Africa offered to release Mandela from jail as long as he promised to renounce violence.

Mandela, though, "refused to do any such thing [.]" Mercer adds that Mandela's "TV smile has won out over his political philosophy, founded as it is on energetic income redistribution in the neo-Marxist tradition, on 'land reform' in the same tradition, and on ethnic animosity toward the Afrikaner."

In 1992, two years *after* Mandela was set free, he was videoed at an event surrounded by members of the South African Communist Party, his own African National Congress (ANC), and "the ANC's terrorist arm, the Umkhonto we Sizwe (MK), which Mandela led."

Courtesy of YouTube, all with eyes to see could now witness "Mandela's fist...clenched in a black power salute" as the members of MK sang their anthem, a little song according to which they reaffirm their pledge to "'kill them—kill the whites.'"

Mandela remained a socialist to the last, Mercer assures us, even though he cleverly—but transparently—"rebranded" it. Mandela's was a *racial* socialism, a point established beyond doubt by the remarks he made in 1997.

Mercer quotes Mandela insisting that "the future of humanity" cannot be "surrendered to the so-called free market, with government denied the right to intervene [.]" Mandela also declared the need for the "ownership and management" of the South African economy to reflect "the racial composition of our society" and criticized "the...capitalist system" in South Africa for elevating to "the highest pedestal the promotion of the material interests of the white minority."

For the conceit of those Westerners who assume that Mandela's thought is a justified response to the evils of apartheid, Mercer has just the treatment. She reminds us that Mandela and his ANC "had never concealed that they were as tight as thieves with communist and terrorist regimes—Castro, Gaddafi, Arafat, North Korea and Iran's cankered Khameneis."

Mercer further reminds us that in addition to once cheering, "'Long live Comrade Fidel Castro!'" Mandela referred to Gaddafi as "'my brother leader" and Arafat as "'a comrade in arms.'"

Moreover, though awarded by President George W. Bush in 2003 with the Medal of Freedom Award, Mercer observes that Mandela couldn't resist issuing the harshest of indictments against America. "'If there is a country that has committed unspeakable atrocities in the world,'" Mandela said, "'it is the United States of America.'"

He added that "'they," meaning Americans, presumably, "don't like human beings.'"

And what is Mandela's legacy to his native South Africa? It is the purpose of Mercer's book to show that it is nothing to write home about.

> Since he [Mandela] came to power in 1994, approximately 300,000 people have been murdered." "Bit by barbaric bit," she writes, "South Africa is being dismantled by official racial socialism, obscene levels of crime—organized and disorganized—AIDS, corruption, and an accreting kleptocracy.

Mercer's book is a rarity inasmuch as it supplies us with a brutally frank account of the real South Africa that Nelson Mandela helped to bequeath to the world. While the rest of the world is busy singing hosannas to Mandela over the next few days, those of us who are interested in truth would be well served to visit it.

REPUBLICANS AND THE CONSERVATIVE MOVEMENT

THERE IS MUCH confusion pervading both the self-professed friends and foes of the Republican Party and the "conservative movement." Given that Republicans currently control Congress, and given that the GOP could possibly regain control of the presidency, there could hardly be a better time for clarity on this score.

For starters, the Republican Party is most definitely not a conservative party. It's rhetoric regarding "limited government" and the rest aside, the GOP is every bit as much in favor of "Big Government" as is its rival. In fact, arguably, it is even more ambitious in this respect, for while Democrats typically focus on "social engineering" here at home—i.e. in an environment to which they are closest and with which they are most familiar—Republicans don't rest here: if the George W. Bush presidency taught us anything, it taught us that under the pretext of "national security" and for the sake of promoting "Democracy," Republicans are interested in engineering societies in far off (mostly Islamic) lands.

In other words, the insult of "RINO" (Republican-In-Name-Only) that traditional Republican voters ascribe to "liberal" Republican politicians isn't an insult at all. Rather, the Republican Party is the, well, RINO Party. To reiterate, Republicans are fans and promoters of Big Government—they are not conservative.

However, there is more.

Not only is the Republican Party not conservative; neither is the so-called "conservative" movement conservative: It is neoconservative. And neoconservatism is a fundamentally different sort of breed than is traditional or classical conservatism.

The Republican Party, with its penchant for growing the national government ever larger for the purpose of implementing domestic and foreign policy prescriptions that are odds with anything that classical conservatives could endorse, is a neoconservative party.

The articles that follow were written with an eye toward revealing the unbridgeable chasm between, on the one hand, the rhetoric and popular conception of the GOP as a conservative party and, on the other, its true identity as the party of neoconservatism.

Neoconservatives, Chris Kyle, and Jesse Ventura

While listening to a "conservative" talk radio show recently, the host—who, along with other Iraq War devotees and, what amount to one and the same thing, "American Sniper" worshippers—brought up Jesse Ventura's lawsuit against the estate of Chris Kyle. I was amazed at the dishonesty of his coverage.

Chris Kyle, "the American Sniper," claimed in his book to have knocked out a man named "Scruff Face" who supposedly had badmouthed American soldiers fighting in Iraq.

Interestingly, it wasn't until he began *promoting* his book that Kyle identified this man as Jesse Ventura.

Ventura has always sworn that Kyle had blatantly lied about the whole incident: Ventura—a former Navy SEAL himself, let's not forget—insisted that he never made the comments that Kyle imputed to him, and there was never any sort of physical confrontation between them. In fact, Ventura didn't even know who Kyle was.

Ventura sued Kyle for defamation.

And he *won*.

Among the wild distortions of my radio host was the claim that the jury was "split." Literally, that's true. But if *80 percent*— eight of ten—Americans agreed on *any* issue, *no one* would claim that they were "split" or "divided." *Everyone* would chalk this up as one issue around which the nation was unified.

Well, 80 percent—eight of ten—jurors in Ventura's defamation lawsuit sided with Ventura.

The significance of this can't be overstated. Among those Constitutional scholars interviewed by *The Minneapolis Star-Tribune,* one remarked that Ventura's case has proven to be "one of the most important First Amendment cases in recent Minnesota history." The reasons for his judgment are not difficult to grasp.

First, because of First Amendment protections, victory in defamation and libel lawsuits are significantly hard to come by. To prove defamation, a plaintiff must establish that *both* the content of the defendant's claims are false *and* that he *knew* that what he was saying was false. In other words, plaintiffs must prove that defendants acted with "actual malice."

Second, since Ventura is a public figure, his hurdle was even tougher than that of most.

Yet he did it: The jury awarded Ventura a little over *$1.8 million* in damages.

Former Navy SEALS, including Terry "Mother" Moy, *the owner of the bar* at which this incident was supposed to have occurred, testified on behalf of Ventura's account, swearing that it never happened.

As Ventura remarked, if this event had really occurred, then word of it would've "spread like wildfire" through the SEALS community. However, Ventura is actually guilty of understatement here: given his high visibility as a public persona, to say nothing of the fact that he was in the town, Coronado, when this incident never occurred precisely in order to *address* a *graduating class of Navy SEALS* at the nearby Naval base, something like this, if it happened, would've become big news—and quickly.

As Thomas Sowell put it not too long ago, juries "deal in facts." And the facts to which this jury had access were not in Chris Kyle's favor.

But there's another angle to all of this that neither the Kyle worshippers nor the Kyle critics are willing to consider.

Let's suppose that Kyle did *not* lie, that every syllable he uttered about his alleged confrontation with Ventura was the God's honest truth. This hardly reflects any better on him.

Think about it: According to the Kyle worshippers, Kyle was over in Iraq fighting for "our freedoms," including and especially our sacred "freedom of speech." This, after all, is the line that his defenders have used against the Michael Moores and Seth Rogens: Kyle fought over there so that they would have the freedom to express themselves here—even when, in doing so, they "trash talk" Kyle and his comrades-in-arms.

Yet Kyle didn't respect Ventura's right to freedom of speech. Rather, once the latter said something that he found offensive, Kyle committed aggravated assault against him.

And then he ran.

Aggravated assault is a crime that carries a prison term of *years*. If Ventura wanted to avenge himself against Kyle, he wouldn't have sued him for defamation; he would've and could've pressed criminal charges against Kyle and *then* sued him for injuries. After all, won't the Kyle-worshippers admit that this is just the kind of thing that a publicity hound like Ventura would do?

Nor would Ventura have to worry about keeping quiet to save face. And this brings us to another piece of unflattering commentary on Kyle if things happened as he said: Ventura could've taken comfort in knowing, and revealing to the world, that he, a veteran in his 50's (at the time) was sucker punched by a guy *23 years* his junior—and over a disagreement on an issue that conflicted the nation.

In any event, Kyle did lie, and he lied in order to profit.

Only blind Kyle-worship—or, to put it more accurately, blind neoconservative ideology—accounts for how anyone could deny this now.

At Last: One Republican Has Finally Got It!

> *The Republican Party is no longer the party of limited government, with limited spending and limited taxes. It is now officially exactly right behind the Democrats—on everything. It is time for conservatives to start looking for a new home. There's precious little left for us here.*

Thus spoke Brent Bozell, founder of the Media Research Center and long-time movement conservative.

Although Bozell deserves two thumbs up for his remarks, it is still worth noting that his epiphany is a little late in the coming: if it was ever really the party of limited government, it has been eons since the GOP ceased being so.

Ron Paul labored indefatigably for decades to call his fellow partisans to their senses, but the self-avowed champions of "limited government" in Washington and "conservative" talk radio ridiculed and derided him.

Just as he spotted the recession of '08 long before it exploded and at a time when his competitors in the presidential primaries insisted that the economy was strong, so too did Paul recognize the identity-crisis in the Republican Party—the chasm between its rhetoric and its policies—years before it dawned upon the likes of Bozell.

It is crucial to bear in mind that it isn't because Paul is so prescient that he has been ahead of the curve on this score. Rather, it is because Republicans have been so blind that accounts for why it has taken some of them this long to appreciate Paul's insights.

The sources of this blindness are probably many. Doubtless, one of them just may be the glare from the contrast between what Republicans espouse with their lips and the policies for which they advocate.

To hear Bozell and others in the conservative movement, one could be forgiven for thinking that the Grand Old Party is just now beginning to retreat from its pledge to promote "limited government." But we needn't go all that far back in time to see that this simply isn't so.

In fact, we needn't go all that far back to realize that the very same voices on the right who have been screaming (rightly, I might add) from the rooftops over obscene levels of government spending and the like for the last four years uttered scarcely a peep over the same during the preceding eight.

Let us not forget that for six years—from 2000 to 2006— Republicans controlled both chambers of Congress *and* the presidency. For six years prior to this, the Republicans dominated Congress. This period supplied a golden opportunity for the party of limited government to practice what it preached while definitively establishing once and for all to the country the intellectual and moral superiority of its ideas over those of its rivals.

Sadly, but perhaps not surprisingly, none of this happened. Instead, Republicans definitively established that all of their talk of "limited government" was just that.

That is, they established to the satisfaction of both their opponents *as well as* a not inconsiderable number of their constituents that they were just as committed to Big Government as were their nemeses. That ever fewer Republicans have showed up at the polls in the last two presidential election cycles proves that long before Bozell had his revelation, Republican voters on the ground got the message loudly and clearly.

But how could anyone not have seen this?

The scope and size of the federal government expanded exponentially while in the care of Republicans under Bush II. Not since Lyndon B. Johnson's "Great Society" had the federal government figured so powerfully in American life. The only difference is that spending under Bush II was even *greater* than that which occurred under Johnson.

Bush II and his Republicans launched two woefully unpopular, drawn out wars. In prosecuting them, he assumed unto the executive branch heretofore unseen powers—like the ominously named "Patriot Act," say—that has left legions of patriots shivering. This is bad enough in itself, but to compound the problem, it erects a dangerous precedent for future presidents to appropriate those very same powers for all manner of evil.

Of course, there is a host of other resolutely anti-conservative policies for which Bush II and his Congress successfully fought. To briefly touch upon only a few, there was: No Child Left Behind (the now nearly universally despised law that increased the federal government's role in education); the Home Ownership Society (which facilitated the explosion of the housing bubble and the onslaught of the recession of '08); Medicare "Part D" (the exorbitantly expensive prescription drug entitlement of '03); and federal funding for embryonic stem cell research (an unprecedented step that only retarded any progress that the pro-life movement could be said to have made).

Bozell is right that "conservatives should start looking for a new home." Yet he fails to see that this is a search that should have begun a long time ago.

Real Conservatism vs. Revolution

The "revolution" that began in Egypt just three weeks ago and that is now spreading across the Middle East has many a Westerner, and even more Americans, smiling. Those who supported

President Bush's "Freedom Agenda" are now crediting the former visionary for setting in motion the domino effect that, they are convinced, promises to bring "Democracy" to the Islamic world.

At this time we would be well served to revisit the thought of the one thinker who is about as widely respected, if not revered, by all self-professed "conservatives" as anyone: Edmund Burke, the recognized "father" of modern conservatism.

Burke was no admirer of revolution. Contrary to popular opinion, Burke didn't even support the American Revolution. It is true that he expressed no shortage of sympathy for the colonists, but he labored indefatigably to persuade them not to sever their ties with the Mother Country.

Burke implored the colonists to resist those "who would alienate you from your dependence on the Crown and [the] parliament of this kingdom." He also went to great pains to remind them that, since the "very liberty, which you so justly prize above all things, originated here," in England, "it may be very doubtful whether, without being constantly fed from the original fountain, it can be at all perpetuated or preserved in its native purity and perfection."

This "liberty" that the colonists "prize" and that is bequeathed to them by England is nothing more or less than the English *constitution,* a constitution, Burke worries, that neither "now, nor for ages," the colonists will be capable of sustaining "in an independent state."

Notice, "the liberty" around which Burke's discussion centers is not an abstraction but a concrete, culturally-specific complex of arrangements that he identifies as the English constitution.

The colonists "are descendants of Englishmen" who, as such, are "devoted…to liberty according to English ideas and English principles. Abstract liberty, like other mere abstractions, is not to be found."

They are also largely *Protestant,* "and of that kind which is the most adverse to all implicit submission of mind and opinion."

Burke tells us that: "All Protestantism…is a sort of dissent. But the religion most prevalent in our northern colonies is a refinement on the principle of resistance: it is the dissidence of dissent, and the protestantism of the Protestant religion."

Burke's political philosophical suppositions are starkly at odds, not just with the views of those of his contemporaries with whom he did battle, but with the abstract metaphysics of most of *our* contemporaries who call themselves "conservative."

The ideas of "Human Rights," "Global Democracy," a "Propositional Nation" and the like he would have found, at the very least (and best), irrelevant to the art of governing.

It wasn't just the violence attending to revolution that Burke abhorred, but the metaphysics undergirding it. He insisted that while he loves a "manly, moral, regulated liberty as well as any gentlemen," he "cannot…give praise or blame to anything which relates to human actions and human concern on a simple view of the object, as it stands stripped of every relation, in all the nakedness and solitude of metaphysical abstraction."

This is a crucial point. No one would anymore think to deny that "liberty" or "freedom" is a good thing than they would think to deny that love is. But precisely because liberty is an abstract concept, it can and does admit of multiple and mutually incompatible conceptions.

The French Revolutionaries who Burke castigated prized Liberty, and contemporary leftists—including Marxists—value it as well; yet *their* idea of Liberty—utopian and, thus, devoid of all context—is obviously eons apart from Burke's. For that matter, Islam too affirms "liberty" as among the highest of goods, but true liberty, as far as it is concerned, is attainable only once Sharia law is imposed upon the whole world. That is, this conception of "liberty" is even further removed from Burke's view than the Marxist's.

As Egypt undergoes its transition to a new form of government, those self-identified "conservatives" who anticipate a new era in the Middle East and the furtherance of Bush's "Freedom Agenda" would do well for themselves to bear in mind Burke's warning regarding "the wild gas" that is "the spirit of liberty." He beseeches us to "suspend our judgment until the first effervescence is a little subsided, till the liquor is cleared, and until we see something deeper than the agitation of a troubled and frothy surface."

Burke reminds us that since "liberty, when men act in bodies, is *power*," and since "the liberty" that the people of Egypt just found for themselves is "*new* power in *new* persons" with "whose principles, tempers, and dispositions" we "have little or no experience," "considerate people" should first "observe the use which is made of *power*" before they congratulate a people for their new found "liberty."

As the world's eyes are fixed upon Egypt and the Middle East, conservatives especially should take their "patron saint's" words to heart.

Center-Left Nation and Neoconservatism

A colleague of mine has drawn my attention to a *Washington Post* blog post—"Why Most Conservatives Are Secretly Liberals"—by a Professor John Sides, a political scientist at Georgetown University.

Sides agrees with fellow political scientists Christopher Ellis and James Stimson, co-authors of *Ideology in America*. Ellis and Stimson contend that America is, at bottom, a "center-left nation," for while "30 percent" of self-described "liberals" are consistent in endorsing "liberal" policy prescriptions, the same sort of consistency can be ascribed to only "15 percent" of "conservatives." And another "30 percent" of "conservatives" actually advance "liberal" positions.

In short, Americans may talk the talk of "conservatism," but they walk the walk of "liberalism." That is, they favor Big

Government.

Sides, Ellis, and Stimson, it seems clear to me, are "liberals."
It doesn't require much reading between the lines to discern this.
That they associate "liberals," and "liberals" alone, with such
virtues as "consistency" and such lofty ideals as "a cleaner
environment" and "a stronger safety net" is enough to bear this
out. Yet in peddling the ridiculous, the patently absurd, notion
that "conservatives" see the media as *promoting* "conservatism," the
verdict regarding their "liberalism" is seen for the no-brainer that
it is.

There is, though, another clue that unveils Sides', Ellis', and
Stimson's ideological prejudices: they equate the term "liberalism"
with a robust affirmation of Big Government. They treat
"liberalism" synonymously with its modern, "Welfare-Statist"
incarnation. There is no mention here of the fact that, originally,
"liberalism" referred to a vision that attached supreme value to
individual liberty, a vision, that is, in which government played,
and had to play, a "minimal" role in the lives of its citizens.

And there is no mention of the fact that, if "liberalism" is
now "an ugly word," it is because the very same *socialists* who
made "socialism" an ugly word hijacked "liberalism" when it
enjoyed a favorable reception and visited upon it the same fate
that they secured for "socialism."

In other words, if Sides himself wanted to be bluntly honest,
he'd have to admit that "liberals" are secretly socialists.

Still, though their premises are bogus, Sides and his
colleagues draw the correct conclusion that most "conservatives"
are nothing of the kind. The truth of the matter is that the vast
majority of contemporary "conservatives" are *neo*conservatives.

Now, "neoconservatism" is a term that hasn't the best
reputation. It has always been controversial, and most of its
proponents have disavowed it to the point of, preposterously,
condemning it as an "anti-Semitic" slur. But George W. Bush and
his party inflicted potentially irrevocable damage upon the label.

"Conservatism" is a more marketable label.

Nevertheless, the reality is that neoconservatism is indeed a distinctive school of political thought. Beyond this, it is fundamentally different *in kind* from classical conservatism. Irving Kristol, the so-called "Godfather" of neoconservatism, an appellation that he readily endorsed, admits this in noting both that neoconservatism exists *and* that "conservative" "can be misleading" when used to describe it.

Neoconservatism, you see, is the invention of *leftists* like Kristol himself. When the Democratic Party began veering too far to the left in the 1960's, Kristol and more moderate leftists began turning toward the Republican Party. *So as to distinguish themselves from traditional conservatives,* they coined the term "neoconservatism."

Neoconservatives, Kristol asserts, are "not at all hostile to the idea of a welfare state"—even if they reject the kinds of "vast and energetic bureaucracies" created by the Great Society.

Neoconservatives endorse "social security, unemployment insurance," and "some kind of family assistance plan," among other measures. But what's most interesting, particularly at a time when Obamacare has divided the country, is that Kristol reminds us that neoconservatives support "some form of national health insurance [.]"

In all truthfulness, however, neither a degree in political science nor an IQ above four is required to know that neoconservatism has always championed Big Government, for it is its *foreign policy* vision more than anything else that distinguishes it from its competitors.

For neoconservatives, America is "exceptional" in being, as Kristol puts it, "a creedal nation," the only nation in all of human history to have been founded upon an "ideology" of *equality,* of "natural rights." The USA, then, has a responsibility to promote this ideology throughout the world.

And it is by way of a potentially boundless military—i.e. Big

Government—that this "ideological patriotism" is to be executed.

Had the foregoing political scientists been looking in the right places, they would be forced to conclude that most "conservatives" are secretly *neoconservatives*.

Is Cliven Bundy a Racist or Just a Republican?

Nevada rancher Cliven Bundy (of whom I've neither written nor said a word until now) was treated as a hero, even a living emblem of the Spirit of the Patriots of '76, by Sean Hannity and many other self-avowed "conservatives" until just a week or so ago.

But it only took a few seconds and a few syllables for this praise to give way to scorn as the inarticulate, media-ignorant Bundy openly contended that far too many blacks today are living under conditions that, in some respects, are far worse than those under which their ancestors were made to live during slavery.

Bundy relayed his thoughts upon driving past a Nevada housing project—"that government house"—and witnessing considerable numbers of blacks just hanging around. "They didn't have nothing for their kids to do," Bundy says. "They didn't have nothing for their young girls to do." This, according to Bundy, is because of the "government subsidy" upon which they depend.

It is this "government subsidy" that explains why Bundy finds himself wondering at times whether blacks today may not actually "got less freedom" than blacks had under slavery. This "government subsidy" accounts for why they "abort their young children" and "put their young men in jail [.]" Contemporary blacks have some of the troubles that they do "because they never learned how to pick cotton."

The reaction to Bundy on the part of his Republican supporters-turned-opponents speaks volumes about the state of the "conservative" movement.

And things are not looking good.

The only difference between Bundy and his Republican critics is that the former lacks both the articulation and media savvy of the latter. Substantively speaking, his position on race is indistinguishable from that which the GOP has been advancing for decades: the social pathology that characterizes the contemporary black lower and underclasses, we are forever being assured, is the product of the oppressive policies of the Democratic Party, policies that substitute a new "plantation," so to speak, for the slave plantations of old.

Clearly, when Republicans describe black Republicans as having left behind "the plantation," the intellectual and moral plantation created by the Democratic Party, they mean to imply exactly Bundy's point: Democrats have imposed upon blacks a form of slavery that, in many ways, is at least as bad, if not worse, than that under which blacks labored for centuries.

Anyone who can't see that Bundy was most definitely not lamenting the old days when blacks picked cotton is either dense or dishonest. It is clear that what he was saying, or trying to say, is that, unlike their ancestors, far too many contemporary blacks, particularly among the youth—the products of the modern Welfare State—lack a work ethic.

For the record, I don't buy this nonsense, but the painful truth is that it is nonsense that *Republicans*—forever desperate to out-Democrat the Democrats by pushing the cult of black Victimhood—have been peddling for years and years before Bundy (inadvertently, for sure) made their reasoning explicit.

Republican "conservatives" reveal themselves as crass, opportunistic panderers when they at one and the same moment talk the talk of liberty and individual responsibility while promoting the fiction of political determinism when it comes to accounting for the scandalous degree of pathological conduct found within black communities throughout the country.

To hear these Republicans (and Cliven Bundy) tell it, the astronomical rates of abortion, illegitimacy, crime, academic failure, unemployment, poverty, incarceration, etc. among blacks are the fault of *Democrats.*

Again, this notion is absurd. And it flatly contradicts the "individualism" for which Republicans *claim* to stand, for it serves to strengthen the ideology of minority Victimhood to which they're supposed to be opposed. Just as individual blacks, and no one else, deserve credit for their good deeds and virtues, so individual blacks, and no one else, deserve condemnation for their evil deeds and vices.

But the point is that if Bundy is "racist" for his remarks, then Republicans are "racist" for pushing the same line. If the latter aren't "racist," but just idiotic and/or dishonest, as I believe, then Bundy too is guilty of the same character weaknesses.

Republicans would be well served to heed Christ's admonition to remove the boulder from their own eyes before proceeding to pluck out the pebble from the eyes of their neighbors.

Conservative Poseurs

Rest assured, there is no short supply of "conservative *leaders*" in Washington and the media who draw their inspiration, not from any moral conviction or passion, but from the hunger to achieve fame and fortune. Such "leaders" or "spokespersons" are mercenaries who have every one of their stakes invested in seeing to it that the base of the movement buys lock, stock, and barrel the narrative that they continue to feed it.

According to this narrative, "conservatives" are the guardians of our "Founders'" dream of constitutional or "limited" government, the lone champions of liberty who are engaged in an enduring struggle with the forces of "the socialist" left who long to swallow up the old Republic in a "cradle to grave" national government.

This epic struggle plays out every presidential election cycle when "conservative leaders" promise us that what we face is nothing more or less than "the most important election of our lifetime."

It plays out on any number of Fox News shows when photogenic panelists with a shared interest in greater publicity for themselves and greater ratings for their network strive to convince audiences that their negligible differences over details are fundamental differences in kind.

It plays out on "conservative" talk radio where the hosts do a masterful (if transparent) job of walking the proverbial tightrope as they aspire to simultaneously persuade listeners that they are both losing and winning the country.

And it plays out in "conservative" publications of various sorts where pseudo-intellectual writers are forever parading out the next Great Idea that will cure the nation of the ills inflicted upon it by "liberalism."

That far too much of "the conservative media" is as shallow as in thought as it is lacking in conviction is readily gotten from any number of examples.

Throughout the first six years of his presidency, George W. Bush's Republican Party held strong majorities in both chambers of Congress. Thanks to his policies, and his disastrous wars in Iraq and Afghanistan particularly, the Democrats not only defeated the Republicans in 2006 and 2008. The former actually gained *super* majorities in the House and the Senate while Bush retired from his second term with a 30% approval rating.

Yet it was no sooner than Bush II was on the road back to Crawford, Texas that "the Architect" of the GOP's defeat—Karl Rove—as well as other Bush lackeys like Dana Perino were signing their contracts to become regulars on Fox News. It is here that such stalwart "conservatives" as Sean Hannity, who daily beats the drums about the Democrats' exorbitant spending, routinely consults Rove and Perino, accomplices to Bush's exorbitant spending, for counsel on how to frustrate the Democrats' exorbitant spending.

It is on Fox that the likes of Bill Kristol and Charles Krauthammer continue to be treated as bottomless fonts of wisdom in spite of their spectacularly checkered track records on all manner of topics.

From the Middle Eastern wars within which we remain mired to the presidential nominations of McCain and Mitt Romney to amnesty for the millions of Third World immigrants that are transforming the character of America, Kristol and Krauthammer have been almost shockingly wrong.

There are numerous other instances that could be cited to show that "the conservative movement" has by and large been taken over by fame-seekers of one sort or other. The most recent of which I'm aware is that of *World Net Daily*.

World Net Daily is a popular "conservative" website whose editor, Joseph Farrah, has rightly ripped into Karl Rove for the faux conservative that he is. Yet Farrah just hired former Pennsylvania senator and GOP presidential candidate Rick Santorum as a regular contributor to WND.

Now, Santorum is about as conservative as Rove. Indeed, if there is any significant difference between the one and the other, or between Santorum and our last president, whose "brain" we are forever told was none other than Mr. Rove himself, I have yet to discover what it could be.

Santorum not only supports "socialized medicine"—i.e. Medicare and Medicaid—but in voting for Medicare Part D, a prescription drug benefit that marked the largest expansion in Medicare since its inception, Santorum actually strengthened socialized medicine while paving the way for Obamacare.

This former PA senator who enjoys the distinction of having lost his bid for reelection by a larger margin than any senator in the Keystone state's history advocates not just "big," but Gargantuan Government. That Santorum actually wants to *increase* our troop presence in countries around the world (the 160 or so countries where we currently have troops stationed isn't sufficient I guess) shows that his foreign policy vision is even more ambitious than that of Bush's.

Among other Gargantuan Government policies that Santorum supported are No Child Left Behind, government bailouts for the airline industries, and Bush's "Home Ownership Society" (that climaxed in the mortgage meltdown and the recession of '08 that gave the country Barack Obama).

Yet Joe Farrah, staunch critic of Rove, has decided to make Santorum an exclusive WND contributor.

Farrah may as well see if the real McCoy, Rove himself, is interested in writing for his magazine.

After all, why go for a replica if you can get the real deal?

Conservatism and War

As Congress and the President debate over whether America should "intervene" in—i.e. launch war against—Syria, self-declared conservatives would be well served to revisit their political tradition's stance on war generally.

Neoconservatism, the political orientation underwriting the anything-but-humble foreign policy of President George W. Bush, is most definitely *not* conservatism—a truth acknowledged unapologetically by none other than Irving Kristol, the "Godfather" of neoconservatism and the person responsible for having given it its name. Classical or traditional conservatism, in stark contrast, is actually quite dovish, even if it is in no ways compatible with pacifism.

Conservatives didn't need Sherman to inform them of war's hellish nature, its death and destruction. That all war entails the killing of human beings, and not infrequently the killing of *innocent* human beings, as well as the destruction of other goods that invest human life with value, does not preclude the possibility of just wars. It does, however, mean that decent people can wage war if and only if all other options have been thoroughly exhausted.

This is the first, and most obvious, reason that conservatives have been slow to enter war.

Secondly, human reason has none of the omniscience that we all too frequently attribute to it. The best laid plans of men often run aground on the unforeseen obstacles that life throws up.

Our intentions have unintended consequences. Whatever our goals, however noble they may be, the pursuit of those goals can easily give rise to evils even greater than those that we're trying to uproot.

In other words, that, say, Saddam Hussein and Bashar al-Assad are bad people who the human race is better off without is an insufficient basis upon which to launch war.

The good combat evil, but they will prevail only if they do so *wisely* or *prudently*. This, conservatives have always known.

Thirdly, the 20th century conservative philosopher Michael Oakeshott noted that since its emergence close to five centuries ago, that peculiar association that we call "the state" has been interpreted in two fundamentally different ways. Some have regarded it as a "civil association." Others have ascribed to it the character of an "enterprise association."

The members of a civil association are joined together by, not a common purpose or shared vision of the good, but a shared "interest" in the preservation of the *laws* that compose their association. Laws, as opposed to *orders, commands,* or *policies,* do *not* tell citizens *what* to do.

Rather, they tell citizens *how* they must avoid acting regardless of what they choose to do.

For example, the law doesn't tell us that we must or mustn't have sex. What it tells us is that *if* we *choose* to have sex, then we are forbidden from doing so *coercively*. The law forbids *rape*. Similarly, the law doesn't instruct us to kill or refrain from killing. It does, though, inform us that if we kill, we cannot do so *murderously*.

In a civil association, there is liberty, for citizens are engaged in the pursuit of their self-chosen ends—not some grand plan prescribed to them by their government.

Conservatives have traditionally favored the reading of the state as a civil association.

In an enterprise association, individuality is subordinated to the common purpose of the association, a purpose in the pursuit of which the government takes the lead. As Oakeshott explains, each person is cast into the role of a servant to the goal or goals for the sake of which the association is held to exist. "Redistributive justice," "social justice," "economic equality," and the like are the standard goals or purposes that we hear most about today.

It is precisely because conservatives have staunchly rejected this understanding of a state that they've been extremely reluctant to embark upon war, for never is civil association more in peril than when a state is at war.

It is during war that everyone is expected to "sacrifice"—i.e. part with their liberty, their time, labor, wealth, and even their very lives—for the sake of "the common good" of "victory." That collectivists home and abroad are well aware of this explains why they are forever seeking to assimilate their pet domestic policies to the language and imagery of war: the War on Poverty, the War on Drugs, etc.

Self-avowed conservatives must take all of this to head and heart as they contemplate interjecting their country into but another Middle Eastern country.

Faux Conservatives

On Friday, January 3, radio talk show host Mike Gallagher charged NSA whistleblower Edward Snowden with being a "traitor" while accusing those of his conservative minded listeners who disagreed with thinking like leftists.

Self-avowed "conservatives," like Gallagher, are, at best, morally confused. At worst, they're intellectually dishonest. Either way, whether they realize it or not, they are accomplices to the left's efforts to "fundamentally transform" Western culture.

Regardless of one's opinions of Snowden the man, the fact remains that he succeeded in calling the nation's attention to a *massive* government surveillance program to which most Americans would have otherwise remained oblivious, a program that enables the government to collect information on citizens while bypassing the Fourth Amendment.

That this gargantuan apparatus—the emblem *par excellence* of just the sort of omnipotent government that our Founding Fathers envisioned with dread, just the sort of liberty-crushing central authority that the Constitution was ratified to preclude—exists, ostensibly, for "our own good," is neither here nor there.

That it exists is, or at least should be, troubling enough for any lover of liberty.

Even if, per impossible, the NSA never abused its awesome powers, even if it had a perfect track record of thwarting terrorist attacks, that it *could* deploy its resources to violate the privacy of American citizens is alone sufficient to paralyze the liberty lover with the fear that his government has betrayed the dream and promise of his forefathers.

The true lover of liberty knows that of which the Framers of the Constitution needed no reminding: there is *no such thing* as liberty.

There are only libert*ies*.

Moreover, these liberties are but the flip side of *the duties* that our Constitution imposes upon *the government*—the *federal,* as opposed to a *national,* government.

By way of its many "checks and balances," the Constitution of the United States codifies a complex set of political arrangements that severely limits both the *authority* and the *power* of the government. Its Bill of Rights was intended to further immunize the citizen against potential abuses of his government.

Interestingly, it is Gallagher and company, not their conservative rivals, who are guilty of allying with the left.

First of all, there is no getting around the stone-cold fact that the term "Big Government" applies to nothing if it doesn't apply to the NSA's surveillance system.

In other words, no one can credibly claim to oppose "Big Government" who isn't profoundly troubled by the existence of the NSA. That Gallagher and his ilk not only support the NSA, but *enthusiastically* support it, proves that they are just *as* prone to Big Government as are Barack Obama and his fellow partisans who also defend the NSA.

Second, Gallagher reiterated today that we remain in *a war.* Note, as long as self-styled "conservatives" insist that we are in a "war" on "terror" or "terrorists," they would have us all think that we are in a war *without end.* Such a notion, infinitely more so than any other, invites endless government growth: nothing is more amenable to Big Government than war.

This "*War* on Terror" that Gallagher and his colleagues unfailingly invoke whenever the government's endeavors to "keep us safe," however constitutionally suspect these endeavors may be, are brought into question is music to the ears of Big Government leftists like Obama.

Under the pretext of "national security," Obama, or any other champion of Big Government, can justify, or try to justify, virtually *anything.* As we've seen, this has already happened with the NSA itself.

This should come as no surprise to anyone who already distrusts Big Government. Think about it: with the exception of anarchists, everyone else accepts that among the legitimate functions of government, providing for the national defense ranks at the top of the list. Furthermore, everyone knows that government has a propensity to perpetuate itself.

Thus, what better way for office holders at the federal level to strengthen and enlarge the federal government than by having everyone else believe that there is a state of perpetual war?

Neither the conservative movement nor the Republican Party promises to make any gains as long as its representatives fail to recognize two things.

First, Americans long ago grew cold on their "war on terror," an interminable government exercise in the social engineering of foreign lands that has already come at the cost of far too much blood, treasure, and liberty.

Second, exactly because of the inexhaustible expansion of the scope and power of the national government that this "war" requires, these voices for "conservatism" and the GOP are actually doing much of the left's work for it as they empower the government further by supplying a catch-all rationale for the project to "fundamentally transform" America.

Dinesh D' Souza's America and the Problem(s) with American Exceptionalism

Its friends in the media would have us think that Dinesh D' Souza's latest cinematic work, *America: Imagine a World without Her,* is worth seeing because of the effectiveness with which D' Souza demolishes the standard leftist charges leveled against the United States. I come away from this film with a dramatically different response.

While D' Souza *is* to be commended for establishing, by way of quite a few tidbits that promise to be news to most viewers, America hardly has a monopoly on "oppression," what he gives with one hand D' Souza takes with the other: D' Souza not only *endorses* his leftist targets' position that America *has* mistreated its racial minorities, particularly those of African descent; he actually—but, doubtless, inadvertently—*underscores* this interpretation.

D' Souza stresses that America is not unlike any other

country or society that's ever existed inasmuch as it is spawned from the same set of circumstances—slavery, war, conquest—comprehensively, oppression—from which all other historical societies spring. In one and the same breath, though, he insists that America is an *idea*.

But if America is an idea—a proposition, a principle, an ideal—then it is most emphatically *not* a historical society. Ideas are abstract and impersonal; the stuff of history consists of concrete actors, individual persons and the communities that they compose.

And since America is allegedly not just an idea, but *the* idea of human equality—equality of rights, or something to this effect—then America is exponentially *more* guilty of the crimes with which D' Souza's left-wing targets charge it.

Consider: If America is alone among the nations of the world in purporting to be the idea (ideal) of (say) "unalienable rights" *incarnate*, as D' Souza maintains, then, at the very least, it alone among the nations of the world has the least excuse—*no* excuse—for *resembling* the nations of the world in engaging in oppression.

So, to the list of grievances filed by his leftist foes against America we can now, courtesy of D' Souza, add those of rank hypocrisy and invincible hubris: hypocrisy for claiming to be the world's messiah while falling miserably short of the ideal that it claims to embody, and hubris for, well, purporting to be the world's messiah.

Of course, D' Souza contends that while America is not unique in practicing the most egregious form of oppression—slavery—it *is* unique in that it waged a "civil war."

Not being a historian, I will put to one side the inconvenient fact that there is no small number of remarkably accomplished historians that reject this grossly oversimplified account of the War Between the States. Familiar as I am with some rudimentary logic, however, I will simply make the following observation.

If D' Souza's narrative is correct and Americans, or the

bearers of "the idea" that is America, *had* to slaughter one another in numbers eclipsing those produced in any of our wars with foreigners in order to abolish slavery, then this reveals that Americans are "exceptional," yes, but exceptionally *corrupt!*

As the black libertarian Walter Williams, among many others, has amply shown time and time again, many societies have ended slavery, but all—with the sole exception of the United States—have done so *peacefully.*

D' Souza's narrative actually paints a most unflattering picture of America, for it distinguishes Americans as the only people ever that, *in spite of* having dedicated their collective being to an abstraction, nevertheless had to savage each other to stop themselves from savaging Africans and others.

D' Souza's position that America is an "idea"—to an even greater extent than most ideological fictions—is a recipe for all manner of disaster.

Those protesting against the unmitigated mess that is our southern border have made signs that read: "Honk if you think the U.S. should have *borders*." If these protestors are remotely as interested in preserving the canons of logical consistency as they are interested in preserving the territorial integrity of America, then they must reject the D' Souza doctrine. The reason is basic enough:

Ideas do *not* have borders.

Once love of country—patriotism—is defined to mean devotion to an abstract, inherently *universal* idea or principle, then geography is rendered morally irrelevant, and maybe even obscene: since anyone and everyone, regardless of where or when they live, can affirm the idea, all who do so *are* Americans.

There can be no moral justification for denying American citizenship to anyone willing to affirm the idea that is America.

D' Souza and his supporters may have given the left the biggest present of all with *America: Imagine a World without Her.*

With Conservatives like This, Who Needs the Left?

National Review Online (NRO) blogger, Reihan Salaam—a self-declared "conservative" who also writes for the left-wing publication, *Slate*—recently charged those who prefer intra-racial dating with being "racist."

Referencing a questionnaire on the dating site, *OkCupid*, Salaam expressed his shock over just how many people *admitted* to having "strong same-race preferences." "One would think," Salaam writes, "that many people who do have such preferences would either choose not to disclose them publicly, or choose to skip the question entirely."

Such people are "clueless," Salaam continues, for "the moral appropriateness" of their practices is questionable.

The idea here seems to be something like this: Same-race preferences (at least when indulged in by whites) are bad because they lead to "in-group favoritism." The latter is bad (at least when indulged in by whites), because *it* leads to "racial inequality."

This in turn is bad, for it is synonymous with "racism."

And, of course, "racism" (at least when indulged in by whites) is the worse.

Government policies designed to combat "in-group favoritism" are bound to fail, Salaam laments, for "in-group favoritism is a powerful human impulse." Thus, it's more feasible for all decent, respectable types to simply aspire to "expand the boundaries of the in-group [.]"

Approvingly referring back to "one of the more provocative Ph.D. dissertations I've ever read"—*The Duty to Miscegenate*—Salaam explains how this can be done.

First, and most obviously, is by way of interracial procreation. He also asserts the need for more "inter-dining." "The rural white Southerner," he remarks, "who dines with nonwhites as a matter of course is doing more to tackle stigma than the urbane white hipster who hardly ever does the same."

Salaam concludes his essay by underscoring that "it's [not] too much to ask those who do express such [same-race] preferences, and those who live them in practice, to reflect on them, and on how there might be more than fighting racism than voting 'the right way.'"

That Salaam's article could make it out of a college freshman course in critical thinking or ethics without being saturated in red ink, let alone be published in a widely read venue (however much of a rag), is a truly scandalous commentary on the intellectual *and* moral state of our culture.

That he considers himself a "conservative," and is so considered by the folks at *National Review* (and beyond?), speaks volumes about the state of contemporary "conservatism."

It should be noted that Salaam nowhere supplies an argument for his thesis that intra-racial dating is "racist." Rather, he stacks the deck in favor of his conclusion from the very outset, and he does so through not one, but two, logical fallacies.

Salaam *begs the question* in favor of his position by *assuming* precisely that which needs to be proved: intra-racial dating is "racist." That his reasoning is viciously circular becomes obvious enough once we relieve it of the mountains of condescending fluff in which it is buried.

It goes something like this: Intra-racial dating is "racist" because it leads to "racial inequality"—which *is* "racism." So, intra-racial dating is "racist" because it leads to "racism."

Yet at one and the same moment, Salaam also resorts to the old tried and true—but logically illicit—tactic of the *ad hominem* attack. Those who disagree with him aren't just in error, and they aren't just immoral: they are *racist.*

Salaam, like every other inhabitant of the planet Earth in 2014, knows all too well that the charge of "racism" serves to simultaneously place the accuser on the side of the angels and the heads of the accused on the chopping block.

There are two other points.

First, if intra-racial dating (at least when practiced by whites) is "racist" and, hence, morally reprehensible, then those of us of racially homogenous backgrounds (at least if we are white) must reckon with the fact that our parents and grandparents were "racist" and, hence, morally reprehensible.

Our very existence is questionable—the legacy of a crime, as it were—for if not for the "racism" of our ancestors, we would not *be*.

Second, it is true that Salaam—a so-called "conservative," mind you, and a writer for *National Review*—does not think that government should intervene to prevent or reduce intra-racial dating. However, this is only because he doesn't think it is *feasible*. In other words, in *theory* he supports such action, but in practice he regards it as an exercise in futility.

This would be frightening stuff to hear coming from anyone's lips. It's that much worse coming from one who is promoted as being a conservative.

The verdict is decisive: if Salaam is any indication of the intellectual and moral fiber of the contemporary conservative movement, the movement is all but worthless.

With "conservatives" like Salaam, who needs leftists?

Neoconservatives vs. Rand Paul

In his July 18, 2013 article, "Rand Paul can never be a mainstream Republican," former George W. Bush speechwriter and *Washington Post* writer Michael Gerson can barely contain his glee over what he perceives to be the Kentucky Senator's fall from grace.

"For a while," Gerson writes, Paul "succeeded in a difficult maneuver: accepting the inheritance of his father's movement while distancing himself from the loonier aspects of his father's ideology." But given recent revelations regarding the "neo-confederate" background of one his senior staff members, Paul "has fallen spectacularly off the tightrope."

Yet his staffer's "disdain for Lincoln is not a quirk or coincidence," Gerson is quick to note.

What he calls "Paulism" demands "more than the repeal of Obamacare. It is a form of libertarianism that categorically objects to 150 years of expanding federal power," the "main domestic justification" of which "has been opposition to slavery and segregation."

From this perspective, "Lincoln...exercised tyrannical powers to pursue an unnecessary war," and the 1964 Civil Rights Act "violates both states' rights and individual property rights [.]"

None of this means that the "Paulites" are "racists," Gerson assures us. However, it does mean that they are "opponents of the legal methods that ended state-sanctioned racism."

Gerson is not yet finished. Paul and his supporters "tend to hate war and federal coercion in any form, even in causes generally regarded as good. They opposed the Cold War and nearly every post-World War II American exercise of power. They equate the war on terror with militarism, imperialism and empire. And they remain unhappy with the War of Northern Aggression."

Gerson's verdict is unambiguous: It is "impossible for Rand Paul to join the Republican mainstream."

Let's simplify Gerson's argument. It goes like this:

Rand Paul's supporters "tend to hate war and federal coercion in any form [.]"

They also tend toward "neo-confederacy" inasmuch as they are "opponents of the legal methods that ended state-sanctioned racism."

Therefore, Rand Paul can never "join the Republican mainstream."

Considered individually, the inaccuracy of Gerson's claims can easily be exposed. The largest problem with his argument, though, isn't the substance of its parts, but its *incoherence*.

If Paul's supporters were the "neo-confederate" quasi-racists who Gerson says they are, defenders of "a regime founded on slavery" and de facto defenders of "state-sanctioned racism," then we would surely have to consider carefully Gerson's admonishment regarding Paul.

And if Paul's supporters really did "hate war and federal coercion" under and any and all circumstances, then, again, the wise would have to take to heart Gerson's counsel against backing Paul.

But Gerson would have us think that these libertarians are *at once* consumed by an inordinate passion for liberty *as well as* an equally inordinate passion for "a regime founded on slavery," a burning hatred for war, the penultimate emblem of coercion, *and* a comparably intense affection for the coercion required by "state-sanctioned" racism.

Paul and his supporters love liberty and they hate liberty. They love coercion and they hate coercion. They are statists and anti-statists.

Gerson's position is what we may call an "argument from the Kitchen Sink," an argument in which the arguer tries to throw everything and the proverbial kitchen sink against his target in the hopes that, eventually, something will stick.

It is also what logicians have long recognized as an argument against the person, the old ad hominem attack.

Whatever name we choose to give to it, Gerson's argument is bad, even pathetic. We should, unfortunately, get used to it, for Rand Paul's rivals—the Gersonians of the Republican Party—promise to haunt us with it in one form or another until Paul has been discredited.

The GOP and the Language of the Left

As the mid-term elections of 2014 approached, it was high time for Republican commentators to walk the walk.

Recently, Mark Steyn, busily promoting his new book, made an appearance on Bill Bennett's radio program. The latter agreed enthusiastically with the former that in order for conservatives to prevail *culturally,* it is imperative for them to prevent the left from assuming control of the language.

Newsflash for Bill and Mark: That ship has long since sailed beyond the horizon.

From at least the time that neoconservatives came to dominate the Republican Party—and perhaps even earlier—so-called "conservatives" have been ceding the language to the left. This, in all fairness, may have not a little to do with the fact that, intellectually and ideologically, neoconservatives are the products of leftist traditions themselves. But the point remains:

Courtesy of GOP-friendly commentators like Bennett and Steyn (and countless others), the left has achieved nothing less than a monopoly on our language.

Examples of this phenomenon are too plentiful to recount here, but a select list should suffice to make the point.

(1) GOP mouthpieces routinely decry "multiculturalism" while insisting that "we are *all* Americans," and yet they never cease to describe, say, *blacks* and *Hispanics* as "African-Americans" and "Latino Americans," respectively.

(2) While paying lip service to the need to secure America's borders, so-called "conservatives" either advocate on behalf of "comprehensive immigration reform"—i.e. *amnesty*—or, if they do *not* explicitly call for this, they nonetheless tirelessly proclaim their

support for *legal* immigration—regardless of the Third World conditions from which it stems.

(3) In championing immigration, Republican media figures can be relied upon to echo the leftist mantra that "America is a nation of immigrants." Few leftist sound bites are as idiotic as this one. And few are as instrumental to the "fundamental transformation"— the destruction—of the country.

(4) GOP talking heads are just as ready to cry "racism" as are their leftist counterparts. Thus, they legitimize the Big Lie that (white) "racism" is an omnipresent threat to everything that Americans hold sacred.

But it isn't just that this is a bold-faced lie; more so than any other device, it is a lie that the left has exploited in the service of facilitating its "progressive"—i.e. its socialist-totalitarian— agenda.

What's even worse is that self-declared "conservatives" don't *just* accuse those *to their left* of being *the real* "racists." They're at least as eager to throw *one another* under the bus at the first sign that one of their own may have made a remark that *could* be construed as "racist."

As for those to *their right*—libertarians and genuine or traditional conservatives—our "conservatives" reserve unmitigated contempt.

(5) What's true of "racism" is no less true of "sexism": neoconservative Republicans, far from debunking it, actually *legitimize* the notion that there is a "war" on women.

Just this week, Rick Santorum was a guest on Michael Medved's radio show. Santorum's rejoinder to the charge that Republicans war against women is a familiar one: it is actually *the left,* with its detestation of traditional sexual mores and avid support for abortion and the like, that *really* hates women.

Again, rather than mock or dismiss the language of the left, faux conservatives accept its terms.

> (6) "Conservative" Republicans remain intent upon invoking the idiom of "rights" when discussing every moral issue—even though this idiom has long been the left's preferred manner of speaking about morality. Leftists know well that abstractions like "human rights" are ready-made to grow government while coercing society into serving their agenda.

In accepting the idea of universal rights (whether they're called "natural," "moral," or "human"), Republicans sanction the moral machinery underwriting the Big Government program of the left.

> (7) Republicans ache for *leaders* in Washington behind whom they can rally. However, the idea that politicians—*government* office-holders—should be *leaders* is a staple of leftist thought. Just the firing of a few neurons goes some distance in seeing why this is so.

First, and most obviously, leaders are expected to, well, *lead.* But lead *who,* and lead *where?* If *politicians*—those with *a monopoly* on both the authority to coerce the citizenry into doing their bidding as well as the power to insure that it does so—are expected to be leaders, then it is to some imagined political promised land or other that they are supposed to "lead" the rest of us.

What this in turn means, though, is that to be effective leaders, politicians must be *visionaries,* aggressive *activists* who

195

compel citizens to part with their property, time, and maybe even their very lives in the service of fulfilling the leader's *plans* for a better tomorrow.

In other words, there is no scheme that is more antithetical to individual liberty than one involving government office-holders who are leaders.

Second, if politicians are expected to be leaders, then the left is right and *politics* trump all other considerations. Culture is secondary to politics. Politics make the world go round, for all that is needed is that we elect *real* leaders.

These are just some examples of how "conservatives" have indeed relinquished the language to the left.

Conservatives and Al Sharpton

"Like draws to like." "Tell me who *your friends are*, and I'll tell you *who you are*."

These are pearls of wisdom, the distilled moral wisdom of "generations and of ages," as Burke has said.

Yet they have been largely trampled underfoot by our generation.

If there's anyone in the world of our national political life that is more loathsome, more contemptible, a figure than Al Sharpton, I haven't a clue as to who that person can be.

Sharpton is an extortionist, a chronic liar, and the worst of rabble-rousers who, through his utterly reckless and racially incendiary rhetoric, has set in motion multiple murders throughout his career.

Innocent human beings have died because of Al Sharpton. More have had their reputations and livelihoods destroyed.

And yet not only is Sharpton a regular guest at the White House, as writer-pundit Debbie Schlussel informs us in, "Hillary Clinton, Rand Paul & Ben Carson Have Something Very Disturbing in Common," some well-known Republicans have ingratiated themselves to Al Sharpton as well.

Ben Carson, Schlussel remarks, had been "given several chances to denounce Al Sharpton" while on *Meet the Press.* Upon alluding to Obama's meetings with Sharpton, Chuck Todd asked Carson whether he believed that the President should be convening with the likes of Sharpton. Schlussel correctly notes that this was "a softball question that anyone with decency and honor would have—and should have—hit out of the park with a, 'Hell no!' and a litany of Al Sharpton's violent and criminal history of race merchantry."

This, though, is not at all how Carson replied. "'President Obama,' Carson proceeded, "should be meeting with lots of people."

In addition to this timid comment, Schlussel reminds us that Carson spoke at Sharpton's National Action Network.

Rand Paul has been even chummier with Sharpton. While meeting with Sharpton to discuss "criminal justice reform" in the wake of the Ferguson hustle that began last summer, Paul made sure to use the occasion as a photo op: more than one picture of Paul and Sharpton shaking hands can be found easily enough on line.

During the taping of the 40th anniversary episode of *Saturday Night Live,* Sarah Palin too posed to have her photograph taken with Sharpton.

The GOP faithful will doubtless seek to justify their idols' reckless decision-making on the grounds that these Republicans are only using Sharpton in order to advance a "conservative" agenda of one sort or another. But there are several problems with this nakedly partisan rationalization.

First, if it is permissible for Republicans to muck it up with low lives like Sharpton for their own partisan purposes—if, in other words, the ends justify the means—then, presumably, it is permissible for Obama and his ilk to share a bed with Sharpton for *their* purposes.

In other words, if we can't draw inferences about the characters of the Carsons, Pauls, and Palins of the world from their association with Sharpton, then it is illegitimate for us to draw inferences about Obama's and Hillary Clinton's characters from *their* association with this vile creature.

Secondly, if it was, say, David Duke, not Al Sharpton, that was the miscreant under topic, there isn't a shot in hell that we'd even be having this discussion. The same ideological groupies—both Democrat and Republican—that spare not a moment to excuse their heroes of choice for cozying up with such a disreputable character as Sharpton would either be as silent as mice or as loud as thunder in waxing indignant.

Truth be told, it is inconceivable that any of the aforementioned politicians, or any others, would come within miles of Duke—even though he isn't nearly as reprehensible a person as is Sharpton (after all, Duke, unlike Sharpton, doesn't have blood on his hands).

Thirdly, it isn't just GOP *politicians* who have been close with Sharpton. Some prominent GOP apologists in the so-called "conservative" media haven't thought twice about associating with Sharpton as well.

Schlussel correctly mentions that Sean Hannity, for instance, has been a featured speaker at Sharpton's National Action Network conferences. Some readers may also remember that not all that long ago Sharpton would regularly appear on both *Hannity and Colmes* and Hannity's radio program.

Bill O' Reilly too hung around with Sharpton: O' Reilly not infrequently featured Sharpton on *The O'Reilly Factor,* and he all but bragged about dining with Sharpton in Harlem.

Like draws to like. Tell me who *your friends are* and I'll tell you who *you are.*

Schlussel provides an invaluable service in reminding us of these nuggets of the moral wisdom of generations while cautioning us against being taken in by wolves in sheep's clothing.

But at the same time, she ought to take care to apply this to herself:

Debbie, you see, used to be a frequent guest on Bill Maher's *Politically Incorrect*.

And while Maher is not quite as disgusting as Sharpton—who is?—he isn't all that far behind either.

Like draws to like. Show me who your friends are and I'll show you who you are.

GOP Failures: Who are the Real Conservatives?

George W. Bush left the White House with an approval rating hovering around 30%. Courtesy of his tenure, and his second term specifically, by 2008 large numbers of conservatives ceased to identify themselves as "Republican," such was their shame.

At least one million of them refused to vote for John McCain. But two years before this, their enthusiasm had already begun to wane considerably, for the Democrats hammered Bush's party, regaining control once more of both chambers of Congress. By 2012, even *fewer* conservatives showed up at the polls to pull the lever for Mitt Romney.

If all of this fails to convince the GOP that it is hemorrhaging its base, the party's leaders would be well advised to look carefully at the comments' sections of *any* number of "conservative" leaning publications—including those that are most friendly to the Republican Party.

The internet has been a great equalizer, the one outlet—the *only* outlet (sorry Fox News and talk radio)—for conservative-minded Americans to give uninhibited expression to their views.

To judge from these views on race relations, immigration, and everything in between, it would seem that perhaps a revolution of sorts is beginning to brew among those whose voice has been marginalized and suppressed by the self-appointed guardians of Political Correctness—both Democrat *and*

Republican.

Yet whether this is a real revolution or not, this much is clear: from the perspective of the great unwashed conservative masses, things are not looking too good for the Republican Party.

In the court of public, on-line opinion, Marco Rubio, for example, has been tried and convicted of traitorous conduct toward both his party and his country for his tireless support of amnesty.

McCain and Lindsay Graham long ago had this verdict visited upon them, but their latest attempt to secure Democrat Party rule in perpetuity via amnesty has renewed with vigor the contempt in which legions of conservatives hold them.

But everyone knows that McCain and Graham are has-beens who've gone as far as they are going to go. Most troubling for the GOP is that its newest line of "conservative" stars is fizzling fast.

Paul Ryan and Chris Christie are as unpopular among the conservative base as is Rubio—and for essentially the same reason: they are viewed as "RINO's." What this really means, though, is that they are regarded as fake conservatives who talk the talk when they need the base of their party but dance with the Democrats at all other times.

Even Rand Paul and Ted Cruz are not above suspicion. The former has made it clear that he supports amnesty—"a pathway to citizenship"—in principle, even if he eventually refused to endorse the specifics of the Gang of Eight's bill. As for Cruz, that he was once one of the architects of Bush II's immigration reform plan back in 2000 is enough to raise concerns. That he hasn't done more to lead the charge against the Gang of Eight's bill compounds those concerns.

Lip service is one thing. Going to the mat against amnesty in the manner in which Rubio and his gang have gone to the mat in favor of it is something else entirely.

The point is this: unless the Republican Party poses a genuine alternative to what the Democrats are offering, its base will continue to erode. The formalities of its platform aside, it has shown itself time and time again to be, at best, but a lighter version—and only a slightly lighter version at that—of its rival.

Amnesty is guaranteed to consign the Republican Party to oblivion. It also promises to expedite the left's agenda to "fundamentally transform" America. Far from being just one more policy among others, nothing less than the fate of our country depends upon it. Why, then, should any conservative vote for a party that wants amnesty?

Yet it isn't just amnesty that is dampening conservatives' spirits. While championing "limited government" out of one side of their mouths, Republicans actively encourage anything but the "humble" foreign policy that Bush II claimed to want back in 2000.

But Big Military *is* Big Government.

Moreover, Americans of all stripes believe that the American soldier, being an *American* soldier, and not a soldier of Planet Earth, shouldn't be deployed around the globe to fight for the sake of some abstract ideal like freedom, equality, or Democracy.

If the party of "limited government" wants to be treated seriously by both their one-time friends and foes, it has got to radically revise its stance on Big Military.

The GOP has some major soul searching to do. Unless it does so soon, its base will continue to shrink.

Anyone with any doubts on this score will have them dispelled quickly enough by the most casual perusal of what conservatives are saying on-line.

GOP Fissures: Is Neoconservatism Breaking Down?

If the Democratic Party's control of the presidency and the Senate can succeed in provoking the base of the GOP to reevaluate its collective political identity, then it all may just have been worth it.

Maybe—*maybe*—the internecine conflict currently on display in the GOP indicates a breakdown of that political philosophy that has dominated Republican Party politics, as well as the so-called "conservative movement," for decades.

The name of this philosophy is *neoconservatism,* and it isn't a version of conservatism at all.

Like their "liberal" or "leftist" counterparts who'd rather die than identify themselves as liberal or leftist, neoconservatives almost always eschew the label "neoconservative." Some have even gone so far as to refer to the latter as an "anti-Semitic" slur.

All of this is as curious as it is preposterous when it is considered that *Irving Kristol,* a Jew and the father of Bill Kristol, editor of *The Weekly Standard,* unabashedly embraced it nearly 40 years ago.

Neoconservatism, Kristol noted, endorse, among other things, a "limited" welfare state of the FDR variety and an activist military that pursues nation-building enterprises abroad.

Neoconservatives, you see, not only haven't any objections to Big Government; they *desire* it, for only a large, centralized government can fulfill the domestic and foreign policy objectives that they want served.

George W. Bush was a neoconservative president. In his second term, Fred Barnes of *The Weekly Standard* had written a book in which he lavished praise upon Bush II for using Big Government for what Barnes described as "conservative" purposes.

This, at bottom, is what "compassionate conservatism" was all about.

Traditional conservatives, i.e., real conservatives, like, say, Russell Kirk—a man, mind you, in whose absence, according to Bill Buckley, the conservative movement in America would've been "inconceivable"—could never so much as imagine that anyone, much less self-avowed "conservatives," could think to speak of a "conservative purpose" of Big Government.

But a traditional conservative is about as unlike a neoconservative as he is unlike a leftist of any other type.

Conservatives have always known that individual liberty is meaningless unless authority is decentralized and power widely disseminated.

It is precisely in the nooks and crannies of our Constitution's numerous "checks and balances" that the liberty of the citizen is to be found. A so-called "federal" government that reigns supreme over the states is not, truly, a *federal* government at all; it is just that sort of *national* or *centralized* government that our Framers dreaded, the sort of government that promised to eclipse liberty.

But that is the government we have now. And it is the government that domestically, as well as and especially, internationally, neoconservatives have helped to create.

Conservatives attach a premium to *tradition*—slow as a snail but blind as a bat tradition. Tradition is nothing but the repository of the wisdom of our ancestors. Political institutions are not chunks of machinery that can be exported anywhere around the globe, but the evolved traditions, the habits, the mores, of a people over centuries and millennia.

Thus, from the conservative's perspective, the neoconservative's crusade, initiated by Bush II, to essentially remake the Islamic world in the image of an abstract ideology— "Democracy"—is beyond foolish. It is reckless. And it is doomed to fail.

Neoconservatives charge conservatives with being "isolationists"—a term that is as baseless as it is meaningless.

Conservatives believe in the necessity of a powerful military, but one that is deployed only for the purposes of prosecuting unavoidable wars and securing its own country's borders. In other words, conservatives insist that the military is never to be used as an agent in a global cause of one sort or another.

Neoconservatives, in glaring contrast, are no different from any other leftist ideologue inasmuch as they have abundant confidence in the power of government to design and implement blueprints (what Fred Barnes and company would call "conservative purposes") for *any society anywhere in the world.*

This in turn also explains why the military can never be big enough for the neoconservative, why any talk at all of trimming military spending is invariably met with the charge that his opponents want to "gut the military."

Yet Big Military *is* Big Government.

Notice, just those Republicans who are now being lambasted as "RINO sell outs"—John McCain, Pete King, Lindsay Graham, etc.—for voting to fund Obamacare and raise the debt ceiling are the most hawkish members of American society. This is a long-standing pattern: the most vocal enthusiasts of Big Military abroad are always enthusiasts of Big Government at home.

These Republican enthusiasts are not "RINOs." They're not even "sell outs."

They are neoconservatives.

Perhaps one good thing to come out of Obama's presidency is that it provides the GOP's traditional base with an opportunity to start discussing who they are—and who they want to be.

www.ingramcontent.com/pod-product-compliance
Lightning Source LLC
Chambersburg PA
CBHW022333280326
41934CB00006B/620